Essential Programming for Linguistics

EDINBURGH ADVANCED TEXTBOOKS IN LINGUISTICS

Series Editors: Peter Ackema and Mitsuhiko Ota

Essential Programming for Linguistics

Martin Weisser

Edinburgh University Press

Edinburgh University Press Ltd
22 George Square, Edinburgh

www.euppublishing.com

Typeset in 10/12 Minion
by Servis Filmsetting Ltd, Stockport, Cheshire, and
printed and bound in Great Britain by
CPI Group (UK) Ltd, Croydon, CR0 4YY

A CIP record for this book is available from the British Library

ISBN 978 0 7486 3855 0 (hardback)
ISBN 978 0 7486 3856 7 (paperback)

CONTENTS

LIST OF FIGURES

LIST OF TABLES

ACKNOWLEDGEMENTS

Before moving on to a discussion of what I consider to be the essential elements of programming for linguistics and why I think that Perl should be our programming language of choice for this purpose, I would first like to thank my students who took the course that this book is based on for their suggestions and criticism of the previous materials. Their input has been invaluable in helping me to identify content that was especially difficult to understand for 'non-programmer' linguistics students and has hopefully helped me to improve the overall quality of this textbook. I would also like to thank the anonymous reviewers of this book for pointing out a few important 'design features' to be included, and Jeffrey Friedl for clarifying an issue concerning Unicode and whitespace handling.

Sample solutions to all exercises and some additional practice materials are provided at the accompanying website of this book at: <http://www.euppublishing.com/page/essential_prog_linguistics>.

INTRODUCTION

This book is mainly intended as an introduction to programming for linguists without any prior programming experience. However, it will hopefully also be useful to students or researchers who have a computer science background and will therefore probably already be familiar with programming concepts, but may have had little experience in understanding and analysing language.

The first question that may come to your mind when picking up a book about programming for linguistics is probably "Why should I need this, anyway?", so I will try to answer this in a few paragraphs. In the days before computerised *corpora* became available for language analysis, researchers or scholars in linguistics either invented their examples – if they adhered to what has sometimes been referred to as 'armchair linguistics' – or they used reference materials collected and stored in the form of filing cards or other means of storage, which they then needed to search through again rather painstakingly each time they wanted to find an example of a particular linguistic phenomenon. With the advent of *corpus linguistics* and its use of computerised data, and especially today's means of accessing these through the internet and other sources, finding suitable samples of language has – at least to some extent – become much easier and it is now possible to analyse and document languages, as well as validate theories about them, much more efficiently.

However, linguistic analysis on such data often goes far beyond what basic search programs for linguistics – so-called *concordancers* – have to offer and frequently involves multiple steps of data preparation and analysis that would be extremely time-consuming – and also potentially very error-prone – if conducted manually. For example, the very first step in analysing data is often to tokenise it, that is to identify appropriate units in the material under analysis and separate the data into them. This is then frequently followed by a stage of morpho-syntactic analysis or *tagging*, and then in turn by a syntactic analysis or maybe a frequency count of specific tagged data in order to conduct genre/variational analyses along the lines of Biber (1988). Now, there may be individual programs available for all these intermediate steps, but chances are that these programs are either not freely available, only run on a different operating system from the one that you are using, require a particular input format or do not produce the appropriate output format that you need to have your data in at particular stages of the processing. In the first two cases, perhaps your only option is to write such a program yourself, and, without any knowledge of programming, in the latter cases you would probably end up manually preparing and correcting your analysis data at each stage of the processing, which would be an especially cumbersome task if the data might change or need to be adjusted in the light of earlier results of your research or changes in the theory that you are applying to the data. Thus, at the very least, it would help to be able to automate part of this process by writing a 'glue' program that runs an existing program, modifies its output according to your specification for the next program, feeds it to this program and so on. If you want to be even more in control of the different stages, then it is probably best to try and write your own program modules from scratch, so that you can then plug them together and control the analysis more easily in the first place.

Another reason for learning how to write your own programs is that you can then design your own experiments for data collection or the simulation of particular features, maybe for testing to see the effects or acceptability of different linguistic processes in certain environments, such as affigation in morphology or assimilation and elision in phonology. And once you have collected some data, there is of course nothing to stop you from analysing it using another custom-made program because existing data analysis programs may not provide all the functionality you need or again require you to convert data into their own specific formats.

As this book is primarily aimed at beginners in programming and people who are more 'language-' than 'computer-minded', I will try to introduce all the necessary concepts step by step, using examples that – whenever possible – clearly reflect their relevance to handling language on the computer, be it in dealing with linguistics problems themselves or handling data on the computer in order to solve these. Based on my experience in trying to teach students of linguistics how to use the computer for language analysis, I know that it is often difficult for 'philologists' to understand all the steps that are necessary for dealing with language in all its different forms on the computer. Perhaps one of the hardest parts of this is to understand the limitations of the computer as an analysis tool, on the one hand, and the complexity of language in its various aspects of ambiguity – such as semantic and grammatical polysemy, on the other – and to devise appropriate steps to deal with these features. In other words, both an understanding of basic storage and retrieval mechanisms and the ability to devise suitable algorithms for tackling the complexity issues just mentioned need to be learnt in order to gain at least some elementary experience in writing your own programs for language analysis. The way I shall attempt to go about dealing with these difficulties through suitable exercises and discussions is twofold and will essentially consist of two different types of 'exercise', one where you will be required to try and understand programming code of various lengths produced by me and the other where, in order to train your algorithmic thinking, I will provide you with a set of instructions to carry out in constructing your own programs. While the former will mainly be used to introduce you to new or more efficient programming concepts and methods, the latter are primarily supposed to help you consolidate your knowledge and gradually learn to write more complex programs by making recourse to what you have learnt in previous sections. Especially this latter type will at times be fairly challenging, and – unless you have a fair amount of prior programming experience – be prepared to spend a considerable time on each exercise before being tempted to consult the solutions contained in the appendix. Most of us 'ordinary linguists' simply cannot learn how to program without a fair degree of practice, so do not even expect to be able to simply read through the book without 'getting your hands dirty' ... In an ideal world, you should even be prepared not only to do all the exercises but also to play around and modify the programs to test different approaches or to experiment with different types of data.

As 'non-programmers' are often not very familiar with anything but the most basic functions of computers, we shall start by introducing a few basic computing concepts, such as using *command lines*, navigating *file systems* and so on, before actually beginning our discussion of programming concepts. Once you can comfortably 'find your way round' the computer without having to rely on a *graphical user interface* (GUI), we shall move on to discussing the most basic programming concepts, such as how to tell a programming language to perform an instruction, how and where to store data while running a program and so on. In Chapter 3, I shall introduce further important basic programming concepts, before we move on to working with actual textual material in Chapter 4, and you will finally learn and practise how to read and write to files in Chapter 5. Chapters 6 and 7 will then introduce you to pattern identification and manipulation, two of the most important options for processing texts and preconditions for many other types of processing. In Chapters 8 and 9 we shall discuss the basic operations necessary for creating vocabulary lists and elementary descriptive statistics in form of frequency lists. Chapters 10 and 11 will then provide you with the necessary means for producing more efficient programs that have a modular structure and also allow for the reuse of individual components in a variety of larger programs. And finally, Chapter 12 is going to introduce you to the design and usefulness of simple graphical interfaces, which often provide the most efficient way of interacting with a user or displaying and processing multi-lingual data.

Having worked through the book, you should not only have learnt about the most essential programming concepts needed for linguistic analyses conducted on the computer, as well as having been exposed to the most useful types of *functions* and *data types* Perl has to offer for this purpose, but also hopefully have developed a sense of how you can go about developing modular resources that should enable you to produce your own analysis methodologies as they may be required for your own particular research tasks.

To make it easier for you to understand where and when I am talking about commands that you need to type in, or specific programming constructs, and so on, I have employed the following conventions in this book. All commands that you need to type in to invoke programs, as well as all programming code, are given in this format. The same applies to the names and samples of programming constructs given in the running text.

An abstract syntax summary for some of the most important program control mechanisms is sometimes provided in boxes with a light grey background and with the abstract information parts in italics, while the programming keywords and brackets appear in a regular, non-italicised, font. Exercises that are not completely walked through in the text are marked by [**Exercise** *number*] in the running text and their solutions can be found under the corresponding entry in Appendix A – Sample Solutions.

Apart from indicating non-standard usage of words or expressions, single quotes outside programming constructs are used to indicate file or directory names, while double quotes are exclusively reserved for direct quotations, in line with linguistics conventions. This also includes a kind of 'simulated reported speech' wherever I try to 'translate' programming jargon and concepts into their natural language equivalents. The important distinction between single and double quotes inside programming constructs will be made clear in the relevant sections. Again, according to convention, at least each first occurrence of a *key term* is shown in italics, as are language samples outside Perl code. On some rare occasions, I also use bold script for **warnings**, where there is some danger of destroying data if you use specific commands without appropriate caution.

1.1 WHY USE PERL?

One of the most compelling reasons for using Perl to do linguistics programming is probably the fact that its original author, Larry Wall, is a linguist himself, and therefore many of the concepts and constructs in Perl are fairly likely to intuitively make sense to other linguists, too. For an interesting discussion of linguistic concepts, such as "topicalization" or "pronouns", by Larry Wall himself, take a look at his *Natural Language Principles in Perl* page at <http://www.wall.org/~larry/natural. html>.

When determining the general suitability of a programming language for the non-commercial user community, though, one of the most frequently cited criteria is that it should be free, which is certainly the case with Perl. Another is the criterion that code should only have to be written once, but should run on different types of machine, in other words be *platform independent*. Perl definitely fulfils this criterion, too, as it not only runs on Windows™ or Unix platforms but has versions for the Apple™ Mac and even VMS, as well as many other *operating systems*. Please note that I am sometimes using the label *Unix* here to refer to both more traditional types of Unix systems, such as HP UX or Solaris, as well as to more modern and recent implementations of Linux. For a complete list of all the different platforms for which Perl has been compiled, consult <http://www.cpan.org/ports/ index.html>.

Many readers may now say "but so does Java™ or Python", to name but two, but, at least in my view, this is not really an argument because Perl is generally much faster than Java and also easier to learn, especially as one can still get by in Perl without having to become accustomed to object-oriented program design, which may initially be very difficult to grasp for the programming beginner and also slower in terms of execution speed (cf. Orwant et al. 1999: 33). Without going into the theory behind objects here, to illustrate the difference, let us take a look at the sample code in Java and Perl for one of the standard first programming examples usually taught in programming books, a simple program that just prints out the message *Hello World!*, starting with Java.

```
class HelloWorld {
    public static void main(String[] args) {
        System.out.println("Hello World!");
    }
}
```

This is some fairly lengthy and perhaps somewhat daunting code, which is largely due to Java's object-oriented approach. The same output, however, can be achieved in Perl with a single line, simply because no object is required for this purpose here:

```
print "Hello World!\n";
```

The latter is also possible in almost the same way in Python, which also – on the surface – allows the user to write the same kind of code as Perl, but when you look beneath the surface it turns out that to do linguistic data processing you are soon confronted with object-oriented features, even when handling such elementary constructs as *words*.

However, this does not mean that Perl does not offer the slightly advanced programmer – such as you will probably be after having read through most of this book – the option to use object-orientation in their program design. I shall certainly introduce and explain objects in Perl in Chapter 11 and will also discuss their advantages in designing larger programs, but until then you will almost remain blissfully unaware of their existence and inherent complexity.

One of the major advantages of Perl is its built-in *regular expression handling*. For the linguist, regular expressions (*regexes*, for short) provide a way of searching for and manipulating similar words/phrases or different groups of words/phrases at the same time and therefore represent an extremely powerful way of analysing and processing them. For example, something like *look[a-z]** used in a regex will enable you to search for occurrences of *look, looking and looked* at the same time. Because of their complexity, whole books, such as *Mastering Regular Expressions* (Friedl 2006), have been written about them, so that this book will only be able to give you a pretty good idea as to what you can achieve by using them, although, no doubt, you will also find them bewildering at times. Again, in many other languages, such as the aforementioned Java or Python, it is at least slightly more difficult to use regexes because you first need to create (*compile*) specific objects before being able to use them.

When many people hear the name Perl, they often associate it with so-called CGI (Common Gateway Interface) scripts, scripts that run somewhere on a web server, and that do not provide a separate interface, other than what is presented on the web page the script is run from. However, it is also possible to create non-web-based user interfaces with the Perl/Tk toolkit, so that Perl can again rival Java and Python in this, only that interfaces in Perl/Tk are often much easier to implement and faster than at least the Java ones. As already pointed out above, we will discuss the creation of simple interfaces in Chapter 12.

Another advantage of Perl is that, in contrast to many other programming languages, you can execute the program code you have written immediately – provided, of course, that it does not contain any errors and Perl is correctly installed on your computer – and without any intervening preparatory steps. This is because Perl is in fact an *interpreted* language, which means that when you call a program you have written, it is executed for you by the *perl interpreter*, which first *compiles* the program, turning it into code the computer can understand, and then runs it for you. Many other programming languages, such as C, C++, C#™, (to some extent) Visual Basic™ or Java, require you to first compile the code into something that the computer can understand in a separate step before you can then execute the program using a different program call. This compilation process may take a fairly long time and you may not always want to have to prepare your programs in two separate steps, especially not if you have only made a minor change to your program. This is why, even though the initial interpretation process may make your program a little slower at start-up, you may still be saving some time using an interpreted language, apart from not running the risk of forgetting to compile some recently changed code again and then being left wondering why your program still shows the same error that you had assumed you had fixed a while ago.

With some of the emphasis within linguistics now shifting away from its earlier 'preoccupation' with – or at least concentration on – English, and the increasing development of national corpora based on the model of the British National Corpus (BNC) – a text corpus comprising 100 million words of modern British English (90 million written and 10 million spoken) – support for non-Latin *character sets* has also become a major issue. Existing practices such as using *transliteration* in order to incorporate short samples of – for example – Greek or other text are no longer a desirable option. This is why any programming language that might be considered suitable for linguistic purposes ought to support *Unicode* in at least one of its implementations. Perl itself does cater for this, either directly through its ability to process *UTF-8* encoded text or by providing mechanisms for converting between different character sets or matching individual characters. We shall discuss some of the issues concerning character sets and so on in more detail in Chapter 5, but will refer to them in other sections of this book, too.

1.2 THE COMMAND PROMPT/CONSOLE

When you begin to design your own programs, you usually do not start by writing fully fledged programs with *graphical user interfaces* (*GUIs*), but small ones that frequently only offer some very specific and also very limited functionality at first. And since we do not usually tend to have a GUI, we need to find a different way of actually starting/running our programs, as well as displaying their output, if one is provided in the form of messages. Usually, at least if you are working on a Windows or Unix computer, this is done by using a *command prompt* or *console*, a small window that allows you to type in a command and execute it by pressing the *Enter* or *Return Key* (↵). From now on, I will use the term *command line* collectively for both the Windows command prompt and the Unix console and only use the more specific terms when talking about features that are in fact specific to either platform.

Programs that are run from the command line are usually *invoked* by typing the program/command name, plus any number of potential *arguments*, that is additional pieces of information the program requires, each separated from one another by a space. One such argument to a program could, for example, be the name of a file to be processed. Let us try using the command line to get a listing of all the files in a particular folder/directory.

If you are working on a Windows system (where I am assuming that you are minimally using NT 4, but preferably XP or Vista), hold down the Windows flag key 🪟 and quickly tap the *R* key once. If you do not have a Windows key, click on 'Start > Run'. This will bring up the 'run' dialogue, where you can type in cmd and press 'enter'. A window with the command line will open and there, you simply type dir and press 'enter' again. This should produce a listing of all the files in the current directory as depicted in the following abridged output.

```
Directory of H:\courses\programming\progs

29-Nov-2008  11:36    <DIR>          .
29-Nov-2008  11:36    <DIR>          ..
03-Dec-2008  19:46             236 coherence.txt
27-Nov-2006  17:06             223 coherence_gap.txt
04-Dec-2006  16:08             433 cohesion_exercise.pl
21-Sep-2006  17:32             480 complex_conditions.pl
13-Nov-2006  16:31             251 copy.pl
16-Oct-2006  16:12             148 first_prog.pl
      .
      .
      .
03-Dec-2008  19:54             422 dir_reading.pl
12-Dec-2008  18:19           1,836 backup.pl
             103 File(s),        73,716 bytes
           5 Dir(s), 3,513,319,424 bytes free
```

If you are using Linux, you need to find a button for the console either on the taskbar or somewhere among the list of programs on the start menu. This may well differ, depending on the exact version of the operating system or window manager you are using. On MacOS X, the console is known as the 'Terminal' and can be found and started from in the '/Applications/Utilities' folder. Anyway, once you have a console window open, the appropriate command to use is ls (for *list[ing]*), followed again by 'enter'.

When supplying arguments to programs, there are different conventions that can be used, depending on the 'platform programming policy' or preferences of the program author(s). On Windows, the specific program arguments to control program behaviour are usually provided by typing a slash (/), followed by the name/initial letter of the argument, whereas on Linux the most frequently used convention is to precede these special arguments by either a single or double dash (- or --). Thus, for example, the directory/folder listing commands, both under Windows and on Unix, can take special arguments. Under Windows, the default output format is relatively 'verbose' and if we want to 'pare it down' to the absolute essentials (that is, only filenames), we can use `dir /b`, where the `/b` means 'bare'. Unix, conversely, is much more frugal with its default output, so if we want to see more file attributes, we need to use `ls -l` (or `-al`), to get the desired output.

Combinations of program-specific and user-provided arguments are also possible, such as `dir /b a*` or `ls -l a*`, which both produce listings of all files that start with an *a*, although there is a difference in *case sensitivity* on the different platforms in that Windows will list all files that start with an *a*, regardless of whether the filename starts with a small (*lowercase*) or capital (*uppercase*) letter, whereas Linux will only list those files that have an initial lowercase letter *a*.

1.3 HOW TO NAVIGATE A FILE SYSTEM

Since at least some readers may never have learnt to navigate a file system 'the old way' using a command line, I will here give a brief – and somewhat simplified – introduction to the most important concepts and commands involved to get you started.

1.3.1 UNDERSTANDING FILE SYSTEM HIERARCHIES

A computer file system is named in analogy to a traditional paper-based filing system using folders or drawers that contain folders, only that the storage medium on the computer is either a fixed or removable *disk* (or other medium), and the data is stored in *bits* and *bytes*, rather than on paper. So, in a sense, you can envisage storing data on a computer as accessing a filing cabinet, opening a drawer, and storing some information in form of a file in it. This visual metaphor is used in GUI-based file management programs, such as Windows Explorer or Konqueror on Linux systems running the KDE (K Desktop Environment) interface.

The filing cabinet in our analogy represents the *root* of the filing system. On a Windows system, this root is usually located on the 'C:' drive, but technically represented by the backslash (\), while on Linux/Unix systems (including MacOS X), it is represented by a forward slash (/). The drawers or folders of the filing system represent other containers below the root, either referred to as *directories* or *folders*. From now on, I shall use the term *directory* only, for brevity's sake. Directories, in turn, can again contain further (sub-)directories and each directory can contain any number of files.

The exact location of a file is given by its *(file)path*, which can be specified either as an *absolute* or *relative reference*. An absolute path lists all directories starting from the file system root to the file itself, each level in the hierarchy being separated from the next one by a *path separator*, which is identical to the symbol marking the root element, that is the backslash on Windows and the slash under Linux/Unix. Thus, if you had a file called 'file.txt' in a 'text' directory contained in a 'temp' directory directly underneath the root, the full absolute path under Windows would be represented by 'C:\temp\text\file.txt' and under Linux as '/temp/text/file.txt'.

Relative paths are only slightly more difficult to understand. As the name implies, when using a relative path, the location of a file/directory is always specified *relative to the current location.* Apart from the path separator, two further 'symbols' are important in specifying relative paths, the dot (.) and the double dot (..). The first always refers to the current directory, whereas the second symbolises the directory immediately above the current one. For the following examples, I shall use the Windows notation to illustrate these concepts, so that if you are using a Linux system you need to replace each occurrence of the backslash by a forward one. Let us assume that we are currently in the 'text' directory within the 'temp' directory and we want to refer to the 'file.txt' file. In order to achieve this using a relative path, all we need to do is to specify the current directory by a dot, add a backslash after the dot and then the name of the file, thus yielding '.\file.txt' as our relative path. However, if 'file.txt' were not actually in the 'text' directory, but we knew that it was in fact one level above this directory but did not really know the name of the containing directory, then we could simply refer to it using this notation: '..\file.txt'. And if it were even one level higher than that, we would use the notation '..\..\file.txt' to refer to it.

The usefulness of these concepts may still not be immediately obvious to you, so let us think of two more good examples where the option of specifying paths in relative terms may be useful. The first one could be a program where the user (or creator) has the option to install it in any location he/she wants to, or is possibly even restricted to installing it in their home directory on a number of different computers. Associated with this program should always be a 'data' directory, where the user can store their data to process, so that the program can easily find it without the user having to navigate through the whole file system all the time. Obviously, since the file structure may always be different on each computer, it would be extremely cumbersome to rewrite the program each time so that it would find the data, but specifying the 'data' directory using a relative path, such as './data/', would easily solve the problem. Perl will understand the / correctly as a path separator, even if you are on a Windows system, so it is probably best to always use slashes for specifying paths, as backslashes sometimes have a special meaning in Perl.

A similar thing applies to our second example, having a complete website that may have to be moved from one server to another, for example if its owner changes jobs. Using absolute links in such a file system structure, where potentially hundreds or more files are linked to each other, would either require a lot of manual rewriting and checking of all the links or actually writing another program to make all the changes for you, which would certainly be a good exercise in programming, but far more time-consuming than specifying all (or at least most) paths using a relative notation in the first place.

1.3.2 NAVIGATING THROUGH FILE SYSTEMS

Earlier, we saw how to create listings of file system contents by using the `dir` or `ls` commands. We can use these commands in order to identify the folder structure of the particular directory we are currently accessing through the command line. Once we are aware of the structure, we can start navigating it by changing the current *working directory* by using the `cd` ('change directory') command, usually followed by an absolute or relative path.

To be able to practise navigating file systems, you need to know about at least one more system command that will allow you to set up the necessary directories. This command is called mkdir (sometimes abbreviated to md), and will allow you to create a new directory using either an absolute or relative path as an argument. Before proceeding, let us first use this command to set up a directory 'temp' and another called 'texts' inside it. To do so, open up the command line if you have not already done so. The default location for the command line to open up in will be your *home directory*, but, depending on the *permissions* you have on the system, you will be able to move into other directories or view their contents. We cannot go into the issue of permissions in too much detail here because it is fairly complex, but if you should run into problems in not being able to access specific directories on your computer or creating new ones, you should either consult your systems administrator, if there is one, or get some advice from someone more knowledgeable, or consult a good reference book on your operating system. At any rate, in your own home directory, you should definitely have sufficient permissions to create and manipulate directories. Before you start creating any, though, first take note of the path specified on the command line before the flashing cursor, the place where you will be able to type in the commands. Especially if you are on a Windows system, you might initially want to write down this location, so that you can return to it again later once we have navigated around a little. Unfortunately, this may differ from one version of Windows to another and Windows does not provide us with a simple option for returning to the home directory. On Linux, though, you can easily move back there by using the cd command without any additional argument or followed by a tilde (~).

To now create the directory and its subdirectory, first issue the command mkdir temp. If you do not get a system error message, this will have created the specified directory in the current directory. You can even verify this again by using the appropriate directory listing command, dir or ls. Once you are sure it exists, change into the 'temp' directory and, this time, type mkdir texts. Of course, we did not really need to move into 'temp' to create the 'texts' directory in the first place because we could have also typed mkdir with a relative path the second time, as in mkdir .\ temp\texts on Windows and mkdir ./temp/texts on Linux, but we did want to start practising navigating, anyway. An illustration of the directory hierarchy we have just created is shown below for ease of reference.

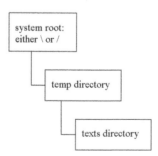

Figure 1.1   The directory structure for practising navigation

As we should currently be in the 'temp' directory and want to navigate into the 'texts' (sub)directory, you can simply type cd texts and press the 'enter' key. If you later want to return to the 'temp' directory again, use cd .. to move back up one level in the hierarchy. If you ever want to move to the root directory, you can type cd, followed by the appropriate path separator. Please note that on Windows, if you want to change to a different drive, such as from 'C:' to your home drive 'H:' on a network, you need to type the drive letter, followed by a colon, and then press enter. I would suggest that, unless you are already comfortable with navigating file systems, you practise navigating back and forth using absolute and relative paths a little more.

Now, having learnt the basics of how to navigate around file systems and to issue commands to the system, we can discuss what we need in order to create our very own programs, starting with a few necessary requirements, such as having an appropriate editor to write the programs in, as well as how to install Perl on your system or at least verify whether it has already been installed.

1.4 PLAIN TEXT EDITORS

When you write programs, you need to pay particular attention to creating files that the programming language you use can actually interpret (or compile). Many users who have never written a program before simply assume that they can write their program *source code* in the word processor they are most familiar with and are then quite surprised if this doesn't work as expected. This problem may be due to two different types of reason:

1. Most programming languages usually require you to give specific extensions to your source code files, such as '.pl' or '.pm' for Perl, and word processors usually use different ones, such as '.doc', and so on.
2. The files produced by a word processor will usually have a specific *binary* or *compressed* format and include specific formatting options, such as **boldface**, *italics*, or underlining, which the programming language will not understand.

The solution to this problem is to use a *plain text editor*, that is a program such as Windows Notepad, or gedit, KWrite, (X)Emacs or Vim on Linux/Mac OS X, or any number of specific programming editors, which will produce files that only contain raw (*plain*) text that can be read by any program that knows how to open and display text files, including word processors.

Which editor you should use is largely a matter of preference and what may be available for the particular platform on which you are working. You can certainly use extremely basic editors like Notepad or any of the other standard text editors provided with most operating systems, but for programming tasks, such as ours, it is much more helpful if the editor provides *syntax highlighting* or maybe even *syntax checking*, where the latter is essentially like a combination of spell-checking and grammar checking in a word processor. And especially if you are planning to work on languages other than English, maybe in order to do a comparative study, it is of great importance that whatever editor you choose should allow you to specify different file *encodings*, particularly some form of *Unicode*, in order to enable you to treat all the data from different languages in the same way. We will talk about this latter issue in some more detail in the relevant sections of the book.

1.5 INSTALLING PERL AND PERL/TK ON YOUR COMPUTER

1.5.1 INSTALLING PERL

In order to execute any programs that you write in Perl or get from someone else, you first need to have Perl installed on your computer. I would recommend that you install version 5.10 but, for most purposes, 5.8 should do as well. As a matter of fact, none of the new features of Perl 5.10 are discussed in this book, but it is still best to be as up-to-date as possible. How you can install Perl will depend on your operating system and possibly also on which version of the operating system you are using. If you are using a Windows system, the easiest way to install Perl is to get ActivePerl™ (from <www.ActiveState.com>), which comes with a Windows installer package. If you are using a form of Unix/Linux or MacOS X, chances are that you will already have a copy of Perl installed. You can test this by typing `perl -v` in a console window, which will not only tell you whether Perl is installed but – if it is – also provide you with information about which version you have. If you do not have Perl installed yet or if you need to upgrade your version, there are various ways to do this, ranging from building it yourself from the appropriate *sources* obtained from CPAN (the Comprehensive Perl Archive Network, <www.cpan.org>) to getting an appropriate *rpm* package for your particular version, if there is one available. If you are not familiar with how to do this, it is probably safest to get some assistance from your systems administrator, as installing different versions may potentially damage other parts of your system if any other applications depend on it.

1.5.2 INSTALLING THE PERL/TK TOOLKIT

The Perl/Tk toolkit is one of a number of different toolkits that provide the functionality for creating GUIs in Perl. I would recommend version Tk-804.028 or later versions of the toolkit, as they become available. If you are using Windows and ActivePerl prior to version 5.10, it is quite likely that it is already installed on your system, but if you are using version 5.10, you may need to install it. To test and see whether it is installed, type `perl -e "use Tk;"` at the command line. If you then do not get an error message starting with "Can't locate Tk.pm", the toolkit is already installed. If it is not installed, there are essentially two different – and relatively easy – ways of installing the appropriate *module*. If you have access to the internet, the easiest way is to type `ppm` at the command line, which will start the *Perl Package Manager* GUI interface. If you type `Tk` in the text box at the very top and press enter, ppm will show you all available packages for the toolkit that are either installed on the system or can be installed or updated. By default, ppm will connect to the ActiveState site to check for available modules, but if you cannot find the relevant package there, you may want to add another *repository*, located at <http://www.bribes.org/perl/ppm/package.

xml>. To add the repository, use the 'Repositories' tab under the 'Edit→Preferences' submenu.

If you need to install the Tk on a machine without any internet connection, things are slightly more difficult. You first need to find an appropriate ppm file (generally Tk-804.028.zip, for the recommended version) to download and later unpack on your local machine. These files may unfortunately be difficult to find but, at the time of writing, I managed to find one in the ActiveState module repository at <http://ppm.activestate.com/PPMPackages/zips/10xx-builds-only/Windows/>. Once you have copied this to your computer and unzipped it to a location of your choice, you can open a command line, navigate to the directory where it is located and type ppm install Tk.ppd to use the command line interface to ppm to install the toolkit. This will copy all the relevant files to your Perl installation, also updating the HTML documentation pages that represent an added nice feature of ActivePerl.

On a Unix system or MacOS X, you can verify the existence of the TK module by typing perl -e 'use Tk;', where the only difference to Windows is that you need to use single, instead of double, quotes. If the toolkit is not installed, it is generally best to obtain the Tk package from CPAN in its source format, unpack it into a temporary directory and compile it yourself, usually by running the following commands in the directory the package has been unpacked into:

```
perl Makefile.pl
make
make test
make install.
```

If you do not get any error messages, the module will have been installed correctly and should be ready for use. If you do get some error messages and are not really very familiar with Unix, you should probably try to get some help from someone more knowledgeable, such as a systems administrator. Having discussed all the preliminaries, we can now finally move on to learning how to write programs in Perl.

BASIC PROGRAMMING CONCEPTS - 1

2.1 HOW TO ISSUE INSTRUCTIONS (STATEMENTS)

A *statement* in programming languages is rather different from what linguists usually understand by statements. It is not a sentence like "This is a book on programming Perl" or something similar, but rather a single line containing one or more instructions written in a programming language and is also – at least in many programming languages – terminated by a semi-colon. The semi-colon makes it easier for the programming language to *parse* its instructions one by one because each time it finds a semi-colon, unless it is found inside a *string* (see variables in section 2.2 below), it knows where one instruction ends and the next one begins.

Let us have a look at a very small Perl program to illustrate this. In order to be able to follow this example better, you should open your editor, type in the program code below exactly as shown there, though without the line numbers and the line break in the third line (which is only there due to limited space on the page), and then save it as 'first_prog.pl'. Once you have done so, open up a command line, navigate to the folder where you have stored the file, and run it by typing the filename and pressing 'enter'. If the ending '.pl' is not appropriately associated with Perl on your system, you may actually have to explicitly run Perl and thus type perl first_prog.pl instead or even provide a complete path to where Perl is installed on your system.

```
1  #!/usr/bin/perl
2  print "This is a book on programming Perl.\n";
3  print "You are currently reading the chapter on \"Basic
   Programming Concepts.\"\n";
```

The first line of the program is usually referred to as the shebang line. This is in fact not a Perl statement but a special type of instruction that is normally only needed on Unix(-like) systems, where it tells the script the location of the Perl interpreter, the program that – as we learnt before – turns your code into something executable. Incidentally, when you read other books on Perl, you will often find authors making a distinction between the language itself, which is spelt with an initial capital letter (Perl), and the interpreter, which is usually referred to in all lowercase (perl) instead. We will follow this convention here, too.

If you should get an error message like "command/file not found" or something along those lines, either your shebang line contained an incorrect path to the interpreter or Perl has not been appropriately associated with scripts that have the extension '.pl'. You could then try to change the shebang line to `#!/usr/local/bin/perl` to see if this works or, failing this, ask your systems administrator where Perl has been installed. On Unix systems, there may also be an issue with permissions concerning the program, in which case you might first have to use the command `chmod +x first_prog.pl`; which changes the file's permissions to make it executable.

If instead you get any messages relating to "syntax error at [. . .] line [. . .]" and/or "Execution of [. . .]\first_prog.pl aborted due to compilation errors.", then there is an error in your program code. In the early stages of your programming career, this is most likely to be a missing semi-colon or a mistyped Perl command somewhere, but do not worry too much if you get lots of error messages initially; even experienced programmers tend to get these quite frequently, and you will learn to avoid some of the more common errors quite soon. The best thing to do when you do get some error message(s) is simply to read the message carefully to find out which line the error (presumably) occurred on, as perl will always try to give you a hint as to where you went wrong. Once you have identified the appropriate line, most editors will in fact allow you to jump straight there to inspect it, often using the keyboard combination `Ctrl + G`. You will also soon find out that, even if you may get lots of error messages in a program, most of them will often miraculously disappear once you have corrected the first one because one error early on in your program may well have an effect on many other parts of the same program.

After this small excursion into what could go wrong with your first program, let us now return to the code shown above. The rest of the example contains the actual program code/instructions. Both of the remaining statements contain one command each, an instruction to display the text, in programming terms referred to as a *string*, enclosed in double quotation marks, following the `print` instruction and up to, but not including, the semicolon. The output of the commands will appear in the command line window. What I just referred to as "the `print` instruction" should really more properly be referred to as the `print` *function*. We will not actually discuss what exactly functions are and how they work until section 10.1, but will initially start using them as appropriate without knowing everything we really ought to know about them yet. Suffice it to say for the moment that a function in Perl – and usually in other programming languages, too – generally requires one or more different pieces of data, referred to as its *arguments*, performs some kind of operation on these arguments, and either passes back a value to the program that uses it or – in rarer cases, such as the one above – simply produces some output.

However, apart from the `print` command, the use of the double quotation marks and the semicolon at the end of the line, there are some other peculiar features in both statements. Let us look at the end of the first statement first. After the full stop, but before the end of the closing double quotation marks, you will see an *n*, preceded by a backslash (\). If you run the program, you will notice that the output text "You are currently reading the chapter ..." starts on a new line. This happens because the character combination \n is a *control sequence*, telling perl to start displaying text on the next line, rather than letting it run on. You can test this by deleting the newline sequence \n from your code and running it again.

If you look at the second statement, you will notice that the double quotation marks within the other set of double quotation marks are also preceded by a backslash. Now, why do we need to do this? Simply because Perl already uses the double quotation marks to indicate that we are using a string, so that whenever it encounters the second quotation marks (before the word *Basic*), it would otherwise interpret them as signalling the end of the string. Because of this problem, we need to *escape* them by preceding them with the backslash, which indicates to the command interpreter that we have a special (*literal*) usage here. You can again try to verify this by deleting the backslash preceding the first double quote and re-running the program to see what happens. This should give you an error message complaining about something called a "Bareword".

Having 'dissected' our first simple program and learnt about some of the most basic concepts, we can now go on to see which kinds of data we can work with and how we can operate on these. If you still feel like experimenting with our first program, though, feel free to play around a little more by changing the output text, adding newlines in other places to break up or align the text better and so on.

2.2 HOW TO STORE DATA IN MEMORY (VARIABLES)

Essentially, when we write a computer program, we are dealing with different ways of handling values, like saving them, editing them, performing calculations based on them, transferring them from one place to another and so forth. Because of the way the computer handles values, we have to have a way of keeping those values somewhere while the program is running, so that they can be stored (either temporarily or permanently), are easily accessible, and can also be manipulated. Whereas permanent storage is normally handled on a *storage medium*, such as a hard disk or CD, temporary storage is in many/most cases handled in the computer's *memory* (RAM), and in order to store information in a particular place in the computer's memory programming languages such as Perl make use of the concept of *variables*, something you are probably already familiar with, albeit in a slightly different form, from mathematics.

A variable in a computer program acts as place-holder for a value – or sometimes also a number of values – with which the program can work. A little pseudo-computer program will demonstrate why this may be needed. Let us, for example, assume that you want to swap two values *A* and *B* with one another and these values are stored in variables by the same name, just for convenience. In real life, we would simply take the two objects and move one from one place to the other and vice versa. However, because the computer handles operations like this in memory in a particular way, what would happen if we did it this way is that when the computer wants to put value *A* into the place occupied by value *B*, the latter would simply be overwritten and therefore be lost. We thus need somewhere to store one of the two values temporarily and for that we would use an extra variable. Let us be original and call this variable temp, and then our pseudo-program would look somewhat like this:

Tell the computer that we want to use a variable called temp.
Move contents of B to temp.
Move contents of A to B's previous location.
Move contents of temp to A's previous location.

Obviously, this program is slightly simplified, as in real life we would also have to tell the program that we want to use two variables that originally hold *A* and *B* and we would also have to put the values for *A* and *B* into them before we can actually swap them. Let us therefore modify our program, so that we have got all the necessary steps in there. The complete program would then look as follows:

Tell the computer that we want to use a variable called temp (and possibly give it an initial value).
Tell the computer that we want to use a variable called A.
Tell the computer that we want to use a variable called B.
Give variable A a value.
Give variable B a value.
Move contents of B to temp.
Move contents of A to B's previous location.
Move contents of temp to A's previous location.

Telling the computer that we want to use a variable is normally referred to as *declaring* it and giving it a value as *assigning to* it. When we assign a value to a variable for the first time, this is called *initialising* it. Perl does not actually force you to declare variables by default, but it is always good practice to do so, anyway, before you start using them. We will later see a way of enforcing the declaration of variables, too, which can be used to make our programs safer and easier to *debug*.

Assignments to variables in Perl are made by writing the name of the variable, followed by an equals (=) sign, followed by the value(s) to be assigned to the variable. What may at first look like equality in a mathematical equation, though, should in fact not be read this way, but rather as "Take whatever appears to the right of the equals symbol and put it into the variable to the left of it!", something that frequently confuses programming beginners. We will see concrete examples of assignments in the next section, when we talk about *data types*, which are the different types of variables available in Perl.

2.3 WHAT TO STORE AND HOW (BASIC DATA TYPES)

When we work on language data, it may initially be tempting to assume that all we have to do is handle letters and words, but this is somewhat misleading. In fact, in analysing language data, we also often need to perform counts of words or sequences, calculate *relative frequencies*, keep track of where we are in the text and so on, for which we may also need different types of numbers. Let us have a look at which data types Perl puts at our disposal and how it handles them.

2.3.1 SCALARS

Whereas most other programming languages make a clear distinction between numerical and 'lexical' variables and also force you to declare them as being of exactly the right *type* for a specific purpose, Perl groups all those variables that can only hold a single value together as *scalars* and gives you a choice as to how you want to use them whenever you work with them. Therefore, no matter whether you declare a variable to either hold a numerical or text value, they will initially look the same, but in most cases indeed behave in a different way when you perform different operations on them. Having just used the term *lexical*, please be aware that, when you read some of the programming literature, this term may have a completely different meaning from the linguistic one there, referring to issues of *scope* that we shall discuss later.

If you use variables as (linguistically speaking) lexical ones – usually referred to as *strings* – you can store individual letters (*characters*), words, sentences, paragraphs or even whole texts in them. You can also combine them with each other to produce sentences out of words and punctuation marks, extract parts of them (for example to identify or strip off suffixes), and so on. If you use them as numerical ones, you can, for example, keep track of positions of words in a sentence by increasing a counter each time you find another word and so forth.

Let us now implement the earlier theoretical example of swapping two variables in order to see how we can work with scalars. Although we now know that they are supposed to look the same, we have not even discussed how to declare them properly. Scalar variables in Perl always need to be prefixed by a $ sign, so that they can be distinguished from the more complex data types we will discuss in later sections. The $ sign is in fact a mnemonic for scalars because it looks like the *S* at the beginning of the word *scalar* if it is written with an initial capital. Alternatively, of course, you could also interpret it as a mnemonic for *singular*, whichever way makes it easier for you to remember the convention. As a matter of fact, this very choice fits one of the basic concepts that is often stated by the Perl programming experts, namely, that *there is more than one way to do it*, which is usually given as the acronym TMTOWTDI and pronounced [tɪmtəʊdi] (cf. Wall et al. 2000: 18).

So, in order to be able to use our three variables A, B and temp, we will have to declare them as $A, $B and $temp. If you forget the preceding $ sign, perl will probably complain to you that it has found a *bareword* or that you are trying to modify a "constant item". Please note that in Perl, all variable names are also *case-sensitive*, so that $a is different from $A, and $Temp and $tEmp different from $temp.

So far, however, we have not even talked about variable naming yet, but it is definitely important to discuss what types of possibilities there are and which things are simply forbidden. From a syntactic point of view, apart from a prefix, such as the $ symbol we saw in the variable names above, the name itself can only start with either a letter or an underscore. Everything that follows may then be a letter, a number or an underscore. Semantically, a variable name should be something telling, something that should ideally enable anyone reading your code to intuitively understand what the variable is used for. Obviously, it should not be too long, either, because you may need to use it repeatedly throughout your code and having to retype something long and complex is quite error-prone, apart from taking longer to read it and making it easier to confuse with other long variable names. However, unless a single, potentially abbreviated word may represent the function of the variable, you should probably opt for a combination of (abbreviated) words, like a noun phrase or clause. Now, as words that run into each other are difficult to read, too, and it is forbidden to use spaces in variable names, it makes sense to either separate the individual elements of the name by underscores, which can 'simulate' spaces, or to start each new 'word' with a capital letter to make them easier to make out. I would generally suggest the first version, but of course this is again a matter of preference.

Initially, we will write our swapping routine to make it swap words and then later modify it to do the same with numbers.

```
1  $A = "there";
2  $B = "is";
3  $temp = "";
4  print "before swapping: $A $B\n";
5  $temp = $B;
6  $B = $A;
7  $A = $temp;
8  print "after swapping: $A $B";
```

Showing the initial, intermediate and final values of the different variables, the swapping procedure would look as follows; greyed out values are still stored inside the variables, but irrelevant for the swapping procedure at the relevant stage because they will either be overwritten in the next step or are no longer used at the end of the swapping routine.

Table 2.1　An illustration of the variable values inside the swapping routine

variable value/content	$A	$B	$temp
before swapping	there	is	
step 1	there	is	is
step 2	there	there	is
after swapping	is	there	is

Now, type the swapping routine (without the line numbers), save it as 'swap.pl' and run it. When it runs, you can see how easy it is to turn a simple 'declarative' structure into an 'interrogative' one by swapping the pseudo-subject there with the auxiliary is.

The first three lines should be relatively easy to understand, as they simply consist of three assignments to scalar variables, where the first two are initialised to some concrete string values and the last one to an empty string. Lines 5 through 7 also represent simple assignments, only this time they are not used for initialising the variables but instead to exchange the values originally contained in $A and $B. Please note that we have also done a few other things here, namely to introduce two print statements in order to display the 'before' and 'after' states (lines 4 and 8). Also note that, although we have declared and initialised $temp separately to an empty string in an extra step (line 3), we could have simply declared and initialised it to the value of $B in one go to save ourselves one step. Perl certainly does allow you to do this, but the way we did it makes it more explicit, which is often better programming practice, at least until you become more fluent in programming.

Lines 4 and 8 also demonstrate another important concept in Perl, namely that of *variable interpolation*. This simply means that you can use a variable name anywhere inside a string and Perl will automatically insert the value currently held inside this variable for you, provided that the string itself appears in paired *double quotes* (" . . . "). This is an extremely handy feature that is absent in most other programming languages, where you first need to join together literal strings and the contents of variables in order to create some similar output.

If you are absolutely sure that you do not want to interpolate anything into a string (or want to even **prevent** interpolation), then you can also use *single quotes* (' . . . '). Please note, though, that in this case, it will also **not** be possible to use escape sequences, such as \n, because they will be interpreted literally! If you want to try this, simple modify our earlier program, 'first_prog.pl', to use single quotes around the strings and run it again. Instead of line breaks between and after the individual output strings, you should now see two literal sequences of \n appearing in the output. And if you do the same thing with 'swap.pl', you will see that, instead of the contents of $A and $B appearing inside the output, you will see the literal variable names showing up, apart from the two output messages now appearing on the same line, with a literal \n between them.

[**Exercise 1**] To see what would happen if we did not in fact use our temporary variable, you can copy 'swap.pl' to 'swap_gone_wrong.pl', delete all assignments that involve $temp and just assign $B to $A and then $A to $B. To practise initialising variables a little more, also change the values given to $A and $B during the initialisation steps to "you" and "are". Before you run the program, try to envisage what the output is going to be.

Now let us return to our correct variable swapping exercise and practise swapping numbers instead of strings. [**Exercise 2**] Copy 'swap.pl' to 'swap_nums.pl' and simply replace the *right-hand side* of line 1 – that is, everything after the equals sign – by 1 and the right-hand-side of line 2 by 2. Note that when we assign numbers to variables, we do not need the quotation marks, as these are reserved for indicating strings. You should also note that, although we have actually initialised $temp to an empty string in line 3, Perl nevertheless allows us to store the number from $B in it. Run the program and check the result.

2.3.2 ARRAYS

The next data type we want to look at is the array. An array is a variable that can hold multiple scalars (or other data types) at once without having to give them separate names. The individual elements of an array are then referenced by the same name + their *index* position inside the array. This is extremely useful if, for example, you have a sentence that you want to *parse* word by word in order to determine which word class each word belongs to. You can start from the first word and move to the end of the array, examining each word in turn and, if the word is ambiguous, you can look at the preceding or following word positions – referenced by the next higher or lower index(es) – in order to disambiguate it.

[**Exercise 3**] In order to learn about how to create and use arrays, let us rewrite our earlier word-swapping program (as 'swap2.pl') in order to perform the syntactic inversion, this time using an array. The way we will write this program is going to illustrate how to set up an array, put some words into it and also how to reference individual elements of the array for retrieving or modifying their contents.

First, we set up the array by creating an array variable. The array variable is prefixed by an @ symbol, where the @ can be seen as a mnemonic for the first letter in the word *array*, so we can call our array @words because it is going to contain words.

```
@words = ();
```

In the line above, we have just declared an array and initialised it to an empty *list* by 'assigning' the empty round brackets to it. Incidentally, you can also use the same assignment to empty an array that already contains values in order to *reset* it to an empty state. In the next step, we are going to put some words into our sentence array, again using the round brackets to indicate a list, but this time with some content.

```
@words = ("there", "is", "a", "linguist", "here");
```

Actually, we could have saved ourselves a step here and declared and initialised the array immediately in one go, without first assigning the empty list to it. In later stages of your programming career, however, you will often find yourself (pre-)declaring variables first and then only using them later on in your code, so it is important to know about how to set up an empty array.

Please note, too, that although the form of the assignment above and the way I have talked about assigning lists to arrays might give you the impression that the two are in fact the same thing, they are conceptually different. You can see this through the fact that you can actually assign a list to another list (of individual scalar variables) without ever using an array. An example for this would be something like ($first_ word, $second_word) = ("good", "morning");, where we assign the word *good* to the scalar variable $first_word and *morning* to $second_word directly, rather than having to use two separate assignments. This is possible in Perl because the round brackets introduce a *list context* (cf. Wall et al. 2000: 69), so the perl interpreter can tell that we are assigning the elements of one list to that of another. The main difference between the left-hand-side list and the right-hand-side one is that the first one is a list of variables, whereas the second one is a *literal* one. Thinking back to our earlier example of the swapping routine, you may now also have realised that I *cheated* a bit with this program in order to achieve a specific learning effect because Perl – unlike most other programming languages – indeed allows you to swap two values without having to use a separate temporary variable. We could therefore rewrite part of the swapping routine as ($B, $A) = ($A, $B); without accidentally overwriting anything.

A very important thing to always remember is that arrays in Perl – just as in most programming languages – are *zero-based*, that is the first index is usually 0, rather than 1.This is a very common source of error but, once you have found yourself accidentally accessing the wrong array element a few times, you will probably get used to subtracting 1 each time from the 1-based position we would normally use in everyday life. Table 2.2 shows which indexes the individual words in our sentence have been assigned to (automatically) when we initialised the array:

Table 2.2   Index positions in the @words array

word	there	is	a	linguist	here
index	0	1	2	3	4

To refer to a single position inside the array, we use the actual name of the array variable preceded by a $ – and **not** an @ – symbol, followed by the index inside square brackets ([. .]). This makes sense because we are really only looking at a *single element* of the array. Something that may initially puzzle programming beginners is that this index may also be stored inside a variable. To refer to the first word in our sentence array, we would therefore use $words[0] to refer to the second one, $words[1], or – if we had previously stored the positions inside two variables $first_pos and $second_pos and initialised them to the same values 0 and 1 – $words[$first_pos] and $words[$second_pos], respectively. Now, you may not immediately be able to see any point in this, but imagine a situation where you might want to skip over one or more elements of an array before you start analysing a syntactic unit to determine whether it is declarative or interrogative and so on, for example, if you have leading adverbs or prepositional phrases. What you would then need to do is first establish where the true beginning of the unit is and then to store this position inside a variable to begin processing/analysing the array from there. Another reason for wanting to use variables to hold the indexes would be if we wanted to extract words from positions of an array of letters/phonemes that we had previously determined based on some other computed criteria, such as only wanting to extract every n[th] letter/phoneme to see whether – hypothetically – it may, for example, be an *e* or a shwa.

Armed with this knowledge about arrays, let us now finish writing our program with the following code, again omitting the line numbers, of course:

```
1  print "declarative: $words[0] $words[1] $words[2]
   $words[3] $words[4].\n";
2  print "interrogative: $words[1] $words[0] $words[2]
   $words[3] $words[4]?";
```

Obviously, this does not take care of the capitalisation we would expect to find in a normal written sentence, but it still simulates nicely how to do a basic syntactic inversion from a sentence array. If not having a sentence-initial capital bothers you, do not worry, we will later find out about ways to fix this in section 4.5. Please note that we have here again made use of variable interpolation, only this time interpolating the array elements by referring to their indexes inside the double-quoted output string. We also interpolated each element of the @words array into the string individually – and manually – which is certainly something we would not want to have to do all the time now, would we?

Apart from assigning a complete list to an array at one time, you can also assign to or change individual elements in an array via an index position. This is done by assigning a value to an array index in the same way as you would assign a value to a simple scalar variable. Thus, in order to change our sentence structure inside the array 'permanently' from a declarative to an interrogative one, we could simply write the following:

```
$words[0] = "is";
$words[1] = "there";
```

Of course, by now we already know a way of shortening the above into a single statement, making use of a list context assignment:

```
($words[0], $words[1]) = ("is", "there");
```

[Exercise 4] Sometimes we may also want to turn an array like @words into a string before doing further processing on it. We have already seen one way of interpolating the array into a string above by interpolating each element individually into a double-quoted string, but there are also two other ways we can use to create a string representation from an array or printing its elements out. The first of these is that we can interpolate the whole array into a double-quoted string immediately. Before we do so, though, let us first test to see what happens if you try to print an array in the same way you would print a string. In order to do this:

1. Create a new file and call it 'print_array.pl'.
2. Set up the @words array as we did previously.
3. Add a print statement with the string "printing the array without interpolation: ". Do not forget to add the space at the end.
4. Add another print statement where the print instruction is followed by @words, a comma, and a newline string ("\n").
5. Run the program to see the output.

The result is probably not what you expected because the array elements are all just printed out joined together without any intervening spaces, which is definitely not what we had intended. In order to fix this problem and see how this is done properly, let us add another line to the program which should read print "printing the

interpolated array: @words.\n";. Once you have added this line, run
the program again to check the new output.

You will notice that Perl will have performed some magic for you here and inserted
spaces in between the different elements of the array, making the output look more like
a real sentence now. However, we may not always want to have spaces in between the
array elements when we 'convert' them into a string. For instance, we may have a list
(array) of words that we want to output one word per line. To be able to achieve this,
we can use one of Perl's built-in functions that is aptly called join. This function takes
two arguments, separated by a comma, a string to be inserted between the different
elements of an array and the array variable itself. [**Exercise 5**] Let us test this again:

1. Create a new file called 'join_array.pl'.
2. Set up the @words array as before.
3. Declare a new string variable $joined.
4. Use the join function as explained above with a newline string and the @words
   array as arguments and assign the result to $joined.
5. Print out $joined.

The output should now consist of the individual words of the array, printed out one
word per line.

By now, we have already seen quite a few operations one can conduct on arrays, but
of course this is by no means all we can do with them. We will later learn about some
other important functions or operations that can be performed on them.

2.3.3 HASHES

Hashes represent another complex data type in Perl. They are like arrays, only that
instead of storing a simple list of values in them you actually store pairs of *keys* and
associated *values*, which makes them ideal for creating data structures like simple *dictionaries* – as they are also called in, for example, Java or Python. You can then use the
keys – instead of using an index as we saw for arrays – in order to look up the values.
You will see this in some exercises in later sections. Hashes are prefixed by the % sign,
so that our sentence could be stored like this:

```
%words = ('word1', 'there', 'word2', 'is', 'word3',
'a', 'word4', 'linguist', 'word5', 'here');
```

A graphical illustration of this hash is presented in Figure 2.1.

Please note that I have here (arbitrarily) chosen names for the keys that do reflect their
positions inside the sentence, as well as the fact that we are dealing with words. However,
I could have equally well just used numbers from 1 to 5 as the key names. A somewhat
more readable – and therefore also more preferable – way of filling this hash would be:

```
%words = ('word1' => 'there', 'word2' => 'is', 'word3'
=> 'a', 'word4' => 'linguist', 'word5' => 'here');
```

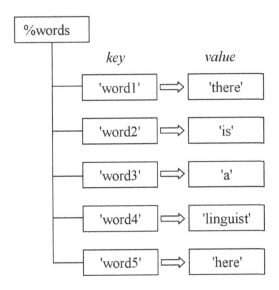

Figure 2.1   A graphical illustration of the %words hash

Here, the relationship between key and value is made clearer, but the => still acts like a comma. To improve readability even more, you can also use line breaks and indentation between the individual key–value pairs:

```
%words = (
  'word1' => 'there',
  'word2' => 'is',
  'word3' => 'a',
  'word4' => 'linguist',
  'word5' => 'here');
```

If you want to declare (and initialise) an empty hash, you simply assign an empty list to it, exactly as you would do for an array, for example %words = () ;. This is because hashes are in fact containers for holding lists, just like arrays, only that they do not hold *ordered*, sequential lists.

Once you have got as list of words (or other values) in a hash, you can simply retrieve them again by referring to their keys. So, provided your program has assigned values to the %words hash as described above, you can now retrieve and print the words via a statement like this:

```
print "$words{word1} $words{word2} $words{word3}
$words{word4} $words{word5}\n";
```

If you remember how we retrieved words from the @words array earlier, this should look almost familiar to you. We are again interpolating values by using the name of the hash (instead of the array this time) with a prefixed $, but this time the 'index' really consists of the key which is enclosed in curly brackets ({ . . . }) instead of the square ones we used for accessing array elements. And obviously, this works the 'other way round' as well again; if we want to assign a value to its associated hash key, we for example write $words{word1} = 'is';.

However, there is one more feature that I have tacitly snuck into our sample code here, which you may not have noticed: although we first defined the hash keys in single quotes when we set up the hash, we simply dropped them for the output and the assignment example given immediately above. This is possible because a hash key in Perl always *has* to be a string, so if the interpreter finds something that looks like a hash key because of its context, it will simply treat it as a string, too. Of course, this will only work if our hash key name does not contain any spaces, but if this is the case, then it can save us some typing, apart from possibly making the relationship between key and value even more obvious.

Now, having to list all the names of the keys 'manually' all the time, as in our example, is a little cumbersome, but we will learn about other, more efficient, ways of accessing hash keys in a later section. Hashes are not only a very good means of saving data structures that consist of key-value pairs consisting of simple scalar variables, such as the *lexical/dictionaries* already referred to above, but can also hold more complex data structures, such as arrays or even other hashes in their value *slots*. We will see some of these uses in later sections when we start setting up some more complex data structures.

[**Exercise 6**] Because hashes are not ordered lists like arrays, you cannot simply use the same ways of printing them out as we did with our @words array. To see what would happen if we employed similar techniques for printing out the %words hash:

1. Copy the contents of 'print_array.pl' into a new file called 'print_hash_test.pl'.
2. Change and adjust the array initialisation to a hash one as shown above.
3. Change all occurrences of @words to %words.
4. Change the earlier print statements from "printing ..." to start with "attempting to print ...".
5. Add another print statement with a string argument that reads "attempting to print the hash using join: ".
6. Add yet another print statement, this time calling the join function with two arguments, a string that contains a space, and the hash variable.

When you run this program, you may be in for a surprise. As you might already have expected from our experience with printing arrays, the first time you try to print the hash without any interpolation, all the key and value elements get printed out without any intervening spaces. You may also have expected that all the keys and their values get printed out one after the other because we know that there is an association between them. Nevertheless, what you most likely did not expect is that the order of the keys is not the same one as you used when you set up the hash. Furthermore, you will notice that interpolating the whole hash into a string will not actually work and instead a literal "%hash" will appear in the output. And last, but not least, you will see that you can use the join function because the hash is a kind of list but – apart from making the output more readable – this will still not give you the right order of keys and values.

Thus, if we would need to guarantee that all key-value pairs should always come out in the same input order again, we know now that we could generally not use a hash, but would probably have to use an array where we always extract two elements at a time to retrieve the pairs. But if the hash does not allow us to do this, then you may well wonder whether it can indeed be a useful data structure for any of our purposes. However, the true power of hashes lies in the fact that we can store the key-value pairs in them in an efficient and compact manner. This way, we can also later dynamically create the entries from values we compute and, for example, use them for counting the frequencies of words. Furthermore, we can employ them to build up many other useful data structures such as more complex dictionary entries out of them, where we will then be able to access specific parts of these data structures via key names that will remain constant for each of the entries we will create and thus allow us to retrieve the information that is associated with them.

Sometimes, you also need to test whether a given key exists in a hash, for example if you have a lexicon of words and their associated grammatical categories that you might want to look up, set, or modify. Especially in the last two cases, it is absolutely essential that you know whether the key already exists because hash keys are in fact *unique*, and thus any assignment to an existing key – or re-initialisation of it – would therefore overwrite any previously existing values! To test for the presence (or absence) of a key in a hash, you can use the appropriately named exists function. We will not actually test this here now because you have not yet learnt how to make use of this information, but we will find out about this a little later.

2.4 UNDERSTANDING ABOUT DEFAULTS (SPECIAL VARIABLES)

Perl also has a number of special variables that refer to predefined constructs, known as *defaults*. These special variables automatically exist for your use without you having to define them because they relate to features the creator(s) of Perl assumed to be necessary for achieving efficiency in programming. These implicit variables often cause problems to programming beginners or programmers who come from a different programming language background. We will only discuss a few of them briefly here and go into more detail in the relevant sections further on, but from now on, you should always try to be aware of their existence.

The first of these variables is $_ (or $ARG) This is known as the default input and pattern-searching space. It is always present when you do processing in list context or when a particular item is currently in focus. For example, while reading in a document line by line, it will automatically contain the contents of the individual line that is being read in, or it might refer to the contents of an element that is currently being read while processing a whole array from start to finish, and so on. Its use will soon become clearer once we start discussing *loops* in a later section.

The next important variable is @ARGV. This holds the space-separated command-line arguments that are passed to the script/program, for example, possibly a number of file names, a word to analyse or a search string to find in one or more documents. We can then retrieve these arguments from the array and process them one by one, making the program more flexible than if we hard-coded all the information permanently. After all, we do not just want to run a program with, for example, the same input file(s) again and again, but instead be able to reuse it with different types of input. Being able to provide arguments for a program at startup time of course also provides the first basis for user-interaction with this program. We will soon find out about other ways of achieving this, too, though.

The last special variable we will mention here is @_. This is somewhat similar to the preceding one, only that it holds the argument list passed to a *subroutine*, which is like an independent little program inside the main one. We shall discuss subroutines in the context of *modularity* later, where we will also learn about how they can make our programs more efficient and safer.

Please note that the shift operator can be used for both retrieving – or actually removing – arguments from the command line array and arguments to a subroutine. Perl will automatically determine whether the context is @ARGV or @_ in this case. Again, we shall see examples of this soon.

2.5 MAKING YOUR CODE MORE INTELLIGIBLE (COMMENTS)

Although we have not even started writing any complex programs yet, this is still a good time to start learning about how to add comments to your programs. These will not only help you to understand your own coding practices better – especially if you have to modify a program you wrote weeks or even months before – but also allow others that may have to take over the maintenance of your programs at a later stage to understand why you have used a particular programming construct to solve a specific problem. You should therefore always try to be fairly concise, but also not too frugal, in whatever explanations you add as comments to your programs.

However, apart from being extremely useful for the above-mentioned purposes, comments can also be used to add other bits of information to your programs, such as when you *created* or *last edited* the program, about who the *author* of the program is, or maybe what the general *purpose* of the program is and which *arguments/ parameters* it might expect. Apart from this, comments can also serve the additional purpose of switching off specific parts of your program temporarily if you do not need them. This may, for example, be the case if you have included a lot of print statements in your code for *debugging* purposes and you suspect that, although you currently no longer need them, they may come in handy again at a later stage.

As we saw earlier, when discussing the *shebang line*, comments are introduced by inserting a(n unescaped) *hash mark* (#) – or *pound symbol*, if you speak American – into your program code. Perl will then ignore anything that follows this hash mark until the end of the current line, which is why they are sometimes also referred to as *line comments*. Thus, if you need to comment out multiple lines, you can simply prefix each line by a #. As an example, I have added a commented version of 'first_prog.pl' immediately below.

```perl
#!/usr/bin/perl
# first_prog.pl
# author: Martin Weisser
# created: 16-Oct-2006 16:12
# last edit: 16-Oct-2006 16:12
# this is the first simple print statement
print "This is a book on programming Perl.\n";
# this is another print statement with embedded,
escaped double quotes
print "You are currently reading the chapter on
\"Basic Programming Concepts.\"\n";
```

And, having now learnt how to add comments to your programs, you should make it a habit to comment to document various aspects of your programs and maybe even 'revise' our earlier examples appropriately to incorporate comments that may make it easier for you to understand what you have learnt at which point on the course.

BASIC PROGRAMMING CONCEPTS – 2

3.1 MAKING DECISIONS (FLOW CONTROL)

In any but the simplest programs, there will be many points at which we need to make decisions as to what our program should do next. Sometimes, these decisions will be based on ascertaining whether there is any data left to process, such as when we want to process all elements in an array and so on. In this case we may have to test for numerical conditions, such as whether we have not reached the final element in the array yet by checking the current index against the length of the array – something we will learn about in the next section. Especially if we are dealing with language data, however, taking actions based on comparing numbers often is not enough and we need a different way of stating our conditions and acting upon them. Well, the way to achieve this is very similar to the way of stating conditions in ordinary natural language, that is, by providing a constraint in the form of an if 'clause'.

Let us see how we can do this by looking at a short program that compares two words, given as command line arguments, to see whether they are equal or not:

```
1  ($word1,$word2) = ($ARGV[0],$ARGV[1]);
2  if ($word1 eq $word2) {
3    print "Both words are equal.\n";
4  }
5  else {
6    print "Words are not equal.\n";
7  }
```

In line 1, we first define two string variables and assign the values of the first and the second command line arguments (cf. 2.4 above) to them, respectively. Remember that all command line arguments are stored in the @ARGV array, so that we can easily access them by their index positions. In order to assign their contents to our variables $word1 and $word2, we use a list context assignment again, as we did for the improved swapping routine, thus being able to assign to both variables at the same time, rather than having to use two separate statements.

In line 2, we use our if 'clause' to specify the condition that if $word1 is equal (eq) to $word2, then we want to execute the print command stated in the enclosing *block* ({ . . . }) that ranges from the opening curly bracket at the end of line 2 to the closing one in line 4. A block in programming is a bit like a paragraph in writing in that it is a logical unit that contains a set of instructions that belong together, such as all the sentences in a paragraph that form one cohesive unit. This means that all the statements grouped together inside the block are only executed if the condition is actually met, and none of them if it is not. Now, despite the fact that in our case, the set of instructions actually contains only a single member (statement), the general concept still holds.

Note that conditions are usually stated in paired round brackets ((. . .)), although there are some special cases where this does not have to be so. When our program encounters the condition in line 2, it tests it using the string *comparison operator* eq and if the condition *evaluates* to true, the corresponding instruction is carried out. If the condition evaluates to false, the program will ignore the block immediately following it and proceed to execute the block that contains the alternative statement that follows the else keyword instead. As the else keyword basically means 'in any other case', it is not followed by any detailed specification in round brackets.

In the context of flow control, it is important to remember that each condition we state/test can only ever evaluate to either true or false, since (default) computer logic is based on a *binary* or *Boolean* system of logic. The following box contains a brief summary of the syntax for 'if-clauses'.

```
if (condition) {
  statement(s);
}
elsif (condition) {
  statement(s);
}
else {
  statement(s);
}
```

In order to test the program now, type it in your editor, save it as 'simple_condition. pl' and run it a few times using both pairs of identical and different words as the two command line arguments. Let us start with a simple example of definite and indefinite determiners, making our program call (perl) simple_condition.pl the a. Now, if you type in what you probably assume to be the same word twice, only once starting with an initial capital letter and once in all lowercase, you may be in for a surprise because the program will tell you that they are not equal. We will soon find out about why this is the case, so do not worry unduly about this at the moment.

If you only provide a single argument to the program, it will quite logically always tell you that the words are not equal because a non-existent word (as the second argument) can never be equal to an existing one. What may come as a definite surprise, though, is that if you provide no arguments to the program at all, it will tell you that the words are equal. This is because – in this special case – our assignment in line 1 has in fact created two 'empty' – or rather, un-initialised – string variables and of course one 'empty' string is just like another. In order to really avoid this problem, we will have to learn something about error handling in a later section, but for now, we can just 'survive' by being aware of this potential problem.

Sometimes, however, we do not only want to test *one* condition and provide an alternative in case it evaluates to false – or even choose not to provide an alternative in some cases. In order to test any number of additional conditions after the first one, we can use the elsif keyword, followed by another condition in round brackets, as shown in the slightly modified version of the program we just wrote:

```
 1  ($word1,$word2) = ($ARGV[0],$ARGV[1]);
 2  if ($word1 eq $word2) {
 3    print "Both words are equal.\n";
 4  }
 5  elsif ($word1 lt $word2) {
 6    print "\$word1 comes before \$word2.\n";
 7  }
 8  else {
 9    print "\$word1 comes after \$word2.\n";
10  }
```

As you can see, the first condition in the modified program stays the same but the second one uses the lt (less than) comparison operator to test whether the first word comes before the second one alphabetically. You may be wondering now how this can be established by using an operator that seems to be purely numerical, but here, we need to remember that characters on the computer are internally represented as numbers, so that a word starting with a letter earlier on in the alphabet will actually be 'worth less' than one with a character that occurs later on in the alphabet. I deliberately said "seems" numerical above, too, when I talked about the comparison operator because lt – just like its counterpart gt (greater than) – is in reality only to be used for string comparison, while the equivalents for numerical comparison would be < and >, respectively.

At this point, it would probably make sense to go on a slight 'detour' into the 'world of encodings' and establish some basic concepts concerning the representation of characters on the computer. For a more detailed discussion, you can consult Nugues (2006: 60–8). Without wanting to go into too much technical detail here, we can simply say that most of the basic Latin(-derived) characters (as well as a number of different control characters) for a long time used to be represented as sequences of *bits* up to one single *byte* (= 8 bits) only on the computer. This made it possible to represent and store up to either 128 (7 bits; 2^7) or 256 (8 bits; 2^8) characters, where each character was assigned a specific number in the original *ASCII* (7-bit) or *Latin1* (8-bit) character sets or their derivatives. Within these character sets, the 'normal' letters of the Latin alphabet are encoded by a single number each, but with a distinction between upper- and lowercase ones, where the uppercase ones range from 65 to 90 and the lowercase ones from 97 to 122. Punctuation marks, numbers and mathematical operators occupy the positions between 33 and 63.

However, there used to be major distinctions between the upper ranges of characters and the individual requirements for them for the different simpler Western character sets, and it proved impossible even to attempt to store the huge numbers of characters necessary for writing in non-Western languages, such as Chinese. This is why additional double-byte character sets were introduced, and eventually the notion of a single character set for all processing needs was devised. This character set is referred to as *Unicode*, which, despite the unifying attempts, still exists in a number of different flavours that use fixed or variable byte length to encode thousands of characters. The flavour we will want to use for this course is a variable byte encoding called *UTF-8*, which stores characters in up to six bytes, but generally has the advantage that the basic Latin characters appear at exactly the same positions as in the simple encoding discussed above, so that opening an English text in UTF-8 would essentially be the same as opening it in ASCII or Latin1. There are actually two different variants of UTF-8, one that includes a byte-order mark and the another that does not. Out of these two, we shall opt for the latter, as an indication of byte-order is generally not necessary for UTF-8 and at least some programs, such as web browsers, do not handle byte-order marks correctly. We will have more to say about encodings later when we discuss reading from and writing to files, but for now let us return to our discussion of 'conditionals'.

If we want to 'negate' the condition, in other words process all data that does not fulfil a certain condition, we can use an `unless` instead of an `if` statement. Let us try another short program to demonstrate this:

```
1  $word = shift;
2  print "You typed the word: \"$word\"\n";
3  print "Program finished.\n";
4  unless ($word eq "finish") {
5    print "Please rerun it using a different word.\n";
6  }
```

In line 1, we are using the `shift` operator to get the first argument given on the command line and to store it in the variable $word. This is actually almost completely equivalent to saying $word = $ARGV[0];, only that it is shorter and can also be used repetitively, without having to specify the exact index inside the command line arguments array.

The reason why I said "almost completely equivalent", though, and not simply "equivalent", is that while the statement $word = $ARGV[0]; would only assign the value contained in $ARGV[0]; to $word, but not actually modify @ARGV, the `shift` operator in fact **does** modify the array by removing its first element, thereby shortening it and moving any potential following arguments forward by one index position.

Please note, too, that we never really did specify an array to `shift` the first element from. The fact that we nevertheless managed to access and retrieve an array element at all is due to Perl's concept of defaults that we discussed earlier. It simply 'knows' that, in the absence of any specifically 'mentioned' array, in this particular context, it has to apply the shift operator to the @ARGV array and to retrieve any values the program may have received at startup from there.

Next, we provide some feedback to the user as to which word has been typed. Since we are interpolating the contents of $word, but actually want to 'highlight' the word by putting it into double quotes, we have to escape these quotes. Of course, we could have chosen other modes of highlighting here, too, but I just wanted to remind you of the fact that you may occasionally have to escape certain characters inside double-quoted strings.

After this, we inform the user that the program has finished (line 3), and only if the last word that was typed in was not the word 'finish' do we prompt the user to restart the program again with another word. Of course, this is only a kind of mock program because we are not really controlling the flow to keep the program itself running, but instead asking the user to restart it instead. In order to be able keep the program 'alive' without any interruption, we first need to find out a little more about the concepts of *input* and *output*, which we will do when we discuss some special types of *loops* in section 3.3.

3.2 DOING REPETITIVE TASKS AUTOMATICALLY (BASIC *FOR* LOOPS)

3.2.1 THE *FOR* LOOP

In the preceding section, we already saw one way of controlling the flow of our program by checking on conditions. This allowed us to follow one particular path in the program, making a decision to perform a single set of (usually different) tasks specified in a block. At the same time, loops in programming are a means of perform-ing the same action(s) – only possibly with slightly different parameters – repeatedly without having to write a statement for each time you want to repeat these action(s). So, for example, if you wanted to add up all the numbers from 1 to 50, you could do this in a for loop like this:

```
1  $count = 0;
2  for ($i = 1;$i <= 50;$i++) {
3    $count = $count + $i;
4    print "$count\n";
5  }
```

What is going on here? We will look at this step by step, each time including the relevant bit of Perl syntax in round brackets after the explanation, but first, copy the above code into a file called 'repeat.pl'. In line 1, we declare a variable to hold the result of our count and explicitly set it to 0 ($count = 0;) to begin with. There is certainly nothing spectacular about this, only that, so far, we have mainly – apart from our little number-swapping exercise – been initialising our variables with strings, and this time we are using a number. This counter variable will later be used to hold the running total inside the loop and end up containing the final sum of all the numbers up to 50.

In line 2, we start a for loop that runs from 1 ($i = 1;) up to 50, each time incrementing a counter variable $i by 1 ($i++;), and for as long as $i is less than or equal to 50 ($i <= 50;). Also note the round brackets that group the individual statements together into 'one' complex statement controlling the for loop. Inside these brackets, we thus essentially have three necessary components: a starting value, a test to check whether a final (ceiling) value has been reached, plus an instruction that states what is to happen with the counter variable each time we reach the end of the block and have to re-evaluate the value of this counter.

Thus, the first time we go through the loop, the starting value – because we have explicitly said so – will be 1. We first test to see whether this is less than or equal to our ceiling of 50, and this being true, we can execute the loop, incrementing the counter by 1 when (or if) we have reached the end of the block. The next time through the loop, the value of $i will therefore be 2, which is still less than the ceiling, and we can again increase the counter, and so forth. Once we have run through the loop 50 times, the counter will be increased to 51 at the end of the loop block, so that the next time we try to run the loop this value will be larger than our ceiling and the test condition will not allow the loop to continue. In case we had any additional statements after the loop block, the program would then continue executing those.

The actual statements that are to be executed repeatedly are listed inside the block, starting from line 2 through to line 5. Inside this block, the essential command is given on line 3, where the current value of the loop counter in $i is added to the current value in $count ($count + $i) and then reassigned to $count, thereby overwriting the previous value contained in $count by the new one.

The statement in line 4 has a dual purpose. We obviously need it for showing the final result of the addition because otherwise we would be doing the addition inside the loop in vain. At the same time, it is also used for verification, so that we can see how the value of $count has increased from one execution of the loop to the next. However, it does not only do that but also demonstrates an important principle in programming, which is that, periodically, one should always check to see whether one's program has actually done the right thing, which can often be achieved via the use of a print statement to output interim results.

Lines 2 and 3 also demonstrate the use of two different mathematical operators. In line 3, we can see how the value in one variable can be added to the value in another simply by using a + sign between them. This is very much like in a mathematical equation, so that it should not be difficult to get used to. The only thing that you do need to remember, though, is to assign the result of the summing operation back to a variable because otherwise it will be executed and lost. The use of the ++ in line 2, in contrast, deserves some explanation because it does not have/require a right-hand-side. Essentially, what we are doing here is telling Perl to increment the value in $i by a fixed value of one each time, so that this is basically only a shorthand for $i = $i+1;, which in turn looks remarkably similar to our addition operation in line 3. The long form again demonstrates nicely that it is usually best to read statements from right to left because this is the way that they are evaluated. This allows us to use the same variable twice, once on the right-hand-side and then on the left, which may initially be a little confusing. Translated into a series of natural language instructions, the long form in this case could thus be expressed as "Take the value of $i, add 1 to it and assign the result back to $i". The $i <= 50; in line 2 demonstrates the use of a compound comparison operator, namely, *less than or equal to*, which is used to test whether the value in $i is still within our range of numbers up to and including 50. The following box contains a syntax summary of the for loop.

```
for (initial value of counter; condition for counter;
increment) {
  statement(s);
}
```

[**Exercise 7**] To practise using simple for loops, as well as to improve our understanding of the way characters are stored at (numerical) code points on the computer, let us write another small program that will allow you to generate all 256 basic characters in the code set that is set up on your computer. Which character set exactly this is will depend on your current code page settings, so the characters you may see at higher ranges may differ considerably.

1. Create another program and call it 'base_charset_loop.pl'.
2. In the program, set up a simple for loop that generates 256 values starting from 0.
3. Inside the loop, print $i, the string " => ", and chr($i), followed by a newline.
4. As we do not know how to store our output in a file from inside the program yet, redirect the results to the file 'charset.txt' on the command line by adding > charset.txt (with a space before the >) after the program name, and test the result by opening 'charset.txt' in the plain text editor.

There are just a few important points we need to discuss here. First of all, a common mistake is to make the loop run for too long, that is up to and including 256, in which case you should get an error message saying "Wide character in print" and the final 'character' that appears in your output file will not actually appear as a single character, but as two. This is because we already have an initial value, the 0, which also stands for a character position, so if you make the loop run up to and including 256 you will accidentally attempt to output a 257th character, which is not part of one of the local base character sets that are generally set up by default. Of course, if your code page should in fact be set up as UTF-8, you would get neither the error message, nor the funny character at the end.

As you may already have guessed, the chr function we are using in line 3 takes its argument, that is the current value stored in $i, and returns the character that occurs at this position in the code page. The other arguments that we pass to the print function, $i and the string " => ", are simply there to make the output easier to understand and possibly to help us look up a particular character again in our text file later. If you ever need to look up the code point value of a particular character, you can use the counterpart to the chr function, which is ord.

Line 4 provides an example of input/output *redirection* that is available in most operating systems that provide a command line. Redirection is generally possible in different ways, such as for *input* (<), *output* (>), or *append* (>>) operations, and to read or write/append to files. For 'quick-and-dirty' file reading or writing, this is generally fine, but we will soon learn about better ways of controlling input and output from within our programs, solutions that will also give us better control over code page/encoding issues.

For loops in Perl are very powerful constructs and we have so far only looked at the most basic options for them, but will introduce further convenient shorthands for them as and when appropriate.

Table 3.1 lists the essential numerical operators in Perl.

Table 3.1   Essential numerical operators

operator	function
+	addition
++	auto increment
−	subtraction
--	auto decrement
*	multiplication
/	division
==	numerical equality
<	less than
>	greater than
<=	less than or equal to
>=	more than or equal to

The basic mathematical operators in Perl behave just like the ones you are familiar with from maths class, so the same rules of precedence also apply. Thus, if you wanted to add 5 and 5 together and then divide the result by 2 and assign it to a variable called $division_result, you would have to use brackets around the addition, like $division_result = (5+5)/2;, as otherwise the result, instead of the expected 5, would be 7.5 instead.

3.2.2   ITERATING OVER ARRAY ELEMENTS

Not only being useful for counting or adding operations like the one we looked at above, for loops can also be used to *iterate* ('step') over the elements of an array, for example, for testing to see whether a given array element fulfils a certain criterion or extracting a specific number or range of words from a text stored in an array. They can also be employed to create so-called *cloze tests*, where every n[th] word of a text is deleted – or rather replaced by a blank – and the test-taker then has to fill in the missing words to make the text coherent again.

To iterate over the whole array, you need to determine the length of the array and then set up a for loop that starts at 0 and runs for as long as a loop counter is less than the number of array elements or as high as the last index position. To determine the length of an array, you can either use the scalar function – as in $array_len

= scalar @words; – or determine the last index position, which can be accessed using the syntax $# + array name, for example $#words in case of our previous word array, and then add 1 to it.

Thus, to control the for loop, you could then either say ($i=0;$i<scalar @words;$i++) or ($i=0;$i<=$#words;$i++). However, for the sake of efficiency, you should only do this if the array you are iterating over is actually fairly small, as calculating the length of the array inside the loop each time makes your program less efficient. A better strategy would therefore be to 'minimise the effort' by pre-calculating the length of the array and storing it inside a variable, as in the example in the preceding paragraph, which would allow us to rewrite the loop control statements more compactly as ($i=0;$i<$array_len;$i++). In order to access the individual elements of the array, we could then simply use the loop counter $i as an index into the @words array to retrieve the current word and process or examine it.

3.2.3 THE *FOREACH* LOOP

We will find out more about the use of operators, including non-mathematical ones, later when we discuss further options for flow control, but first, let us look at a special type of for loop, the foreach loop. This type of loop allows you to *iterate* over a list of values, for example all the elements of an array, without having to explicitly specify a condition or counter variable. Let us see how this would work with our earlier sentence array:

```
1  @words = split / /, "there is a linguist here";
2  foreach $word (@words) {
3    print "$word\n";
4  }
```

In line 1, we again set up our sentence array, but this time in a more practical manner, that is by using Perl's built-in split function. The split function cuts a string into multiple parts, depending on the delimiter used, in other words whatever we want to specify as separating the individual elements from each other. In our case, the delimiter (given between forward slashes) is simply a space. In line 2, we start a foreach loop iterating over the @words array (given in round brackets), setting each element of the array to the variable $word as we go through it. Please note that we do not even have to specify $word as our variable (simply writing foreach (@ words)), in which case each element of the array would automatically be assigned to the $_ default variable discussed earlier in the section on defaults. Inside the loop, we simply print out every word in the array, followed by a newline. If we had not specified $word as our variable, we would have also had to write print "$_\n";. The following box contains a summary of the syntax of the foreach loop.

```
foreach element (list/array) {
  statement(s);
}
```

Not having to set up a counter variable and checking on the length of the array, and so on, to ensure that we do not get any index positions wrong and accidentally print less than the array contains is highly useful and can save us a lot of typing. Whenever possible, you should therefore try and use a foreach loop to process all the elements contained in an array. However, there are also cases when you will need to use index positions, and thus a counter-driven loop. In order to practise using both types of loops, let us now try to implement the scenario we envisaged earlier, where we wanted to extract every n^{th} letter from a string of words/characters to see whether it might be an *e*. The way we will implement this program – called 'extract_nth_element. pl' – certainly is not the most efficient way we could implement it in Perl, but at least we already know enough to achieve the result we want.

Before we start implementing our example, though, let us first spend some time thinking about the steps we need to take in order to achieve our goal and the issues that may be involved in doing so. Because we do not know how to read in longer text strings from files yet we will have to simulate a sufficiently long string by using a simple string variable. Next, we need to find a way to treat the string as a series of characters, which means that we have to split it into those characters somehow and to store the result in a convenient list form, generally an array.

Now, normal texts also contain spaces between the words, which count as characters on the computer, but not actually for humans, so we need to find a way to get rid of those when we process our series of characters for our purpose. The easiest way for us to do this at the moment is to process each element of our list of characters in turn, examine it to see whether it is a space or not, and only save the actual letters to a new list. Once we have the final list of characters, which we would naturally want to store inside another array, we would then like to extract every n^{th} element from the array and examine it to see whether it was an *e*. As we know, though, arrays are 0-based, so we first need to translate the index position to a 'real-life index' by adding one to it and then divide it by n to see whether there is a remainder. If the translated index position is 'cleanly' divisible by n, then we can extract the element at the untranslated index position and store it in another array to hold our results in order to display them later for verification purposes.

However, and more importantly, in order to be able to prove or disprove our hypothesis, we also need to test whether the character is an *e* and, if so, record this using a counter variable that we can print out – together with a meaningful message – at the end of our program. There are some more, but smaller problems we need to solve in the process, but we will try to discuss these in conjunction with the following implementation.

```
1  $n = shift;
2  $counter = 0;
3  $string = 'this is a fairly long test string to
   test the hypothesis that every nth letter inside
   this string may be an e';
4  print "test string: ",$string,"\n";
5  # split the string into its individual characters
```

```perl
 6  @original_array = split //, $string;
 7  @array_wo_spaces = ();
 8  @results = ();
 9  # print for debugging purposes to test whether
    splitting was successful
10  #print join("|", @original_array),"\n";
11  # remove spaces the inefficient way
12  foreach $letter (@original_array) {
13      if ($letter ne ' ') {
14        push @array_wo_spaces, $letter;
15      }
16  }
17  # debugging output again
18  #print join("|", @array_wo_spaces),"\n";
19  # test loop
20  $array_len = scalar @array_wo_spaces;
21  for ($i=0;$i<$array_len;$i++) {
22      if (($i+1)%$n == 0) {
23        push @results, $array_wo_spaces[$i];
24        if ($array_wo_spaces[$i] eq 'e') {
25          $counter++;
26        }
27      }
28  }
29  print "here are the results for n = $n:\t";
30  print join "-", @results;
31  $ordinal = "";
32  if ($n == 1) {
33      $ordinal = "${n}st";
34  }
35  elsif ($n == 2) {
36      $ordinal = "${n}nd";
37  }
38  elsif ($n == 3) {
39      $ordinal = "${n}rd";
40  }
41  else {
42      $ordinal = "${n}th";
43  }
44  print "\n$counter 'e's found in every $ordinal
    position in a string of length ", scalar(
    @array_wo_spaces);
```

The code above may be a bit daunting to you because it probably represents the first fairly long program you have ever had to deal with, but you should soon notice that it consists of a series of steps that are frequently very similar in nature so that, altogether, there is not actually too much in it that is new to you. I have also added a number of comments to the code to make it easier to understand what is going on where.

In the first three lines, we retrieve a value for n from the command line and assign it to $n, initialise the counter variable $counter to 0, and define a string variable $string to simulate our text. Just in case we should want to modify the string later, maybe providing it as a second command line argument, and to help us remember which string exactly we chose, we print it out for reference in line 4.

Line 5 is just a comment, explaining what happens in line 6. There, we make use of a special feature of the split function that allows us to split a string into its individual characters if we provide an empty delimiter, that is the double slashes without anything in between them. The result is assigned to an array of characters called @original_array. Next, in lines 7 and 8, we set up two more empty arrays, called @array_wo_spaces – where *wo* obviously is an abbreviation for *without* – and @results. The first one is going to hold a copy of the original character array, but without the spaces, and the second one will be used for storing every nth character to be extracted from the former.

Lines 9 and 10 contain a comment and a debugging statement that, when uncommented, will print out the original character array just to prove that the splitting has really worked as planned. Both lines are obviously not needed once the program has been finalised and tested, but I left them in to allow you to test the interim progress. As we have done previously, we here use the join function with a pipe symbol as delimiter/'joiner' to make it easier to see the individual elements of the array once we have passed its result to the print function.

The next line (11) simply serves as a reminder that our next few steps will be taken to eliminate the spaces from the original array and store a copy in @array_wo_spaces. In lines 12–16, we iterate over all the elements of the original array, test to see whether the current character in $letter is not (equal to) a space ($letter ne ' ') and, if so, append (push) it to the end of the array without spaces.

Lines 17 and 18 are for debugging output again, just like we saw for 9 and 10, and line 19 is simply a comment telling us that the actual loop for testing starts from this point.

In lines 20–28, we do the real 'hard work'. We first calculate the length of the spaceless array and then run a for loop iterating over all of its index positions. Next, we test to see whether the remainder of the division by $n of the 'translated' index position is 0, and if the division is clean we push the character at the current index position onto the end of the results array. Lines 24–26 also contain another test to establish whether the character at the current index position is actually an *e* and, that being the case, we increase the value inside the counter variable by one.

The next two lines (29–30) are used to give us an indication of the results of the test and a reminder of what $n actually was. For printing out the array, we use a hyphen as a delimiter this time to separate the individual elements of the results array.

Lines 31–43 are used to create a sensible ordinal representation for n in our final message to the user. In order to achieve this, we use another variable, $ordinal, and, depending on whether the value of $n is a 1, 2, 3, or anything else, we create a new string, to be stored in $ordinal, which creates a correct ordinal representation *1st, 2nd, 3rd, 4th* ... Please note, though, that we cannot completely handle *n*s above 10 in this way, but this would not really make much sense in our test, anyway, because we would assume n to be fairly small or otherwise we would probably be researching a fairly uninteresting phenomenon. There is also one more special thing in the way that we interpolate $n into $ordinal: we need to surround the *n* of $n by curly brackets because otherwise Perl would assume that we have some strange, undefined variables called $nst, $nnd, $nrd, and $nth in our code because it cannot distinguish between the end of $n and the next character(s) ... We will soon learn about a way in which we can avoid this problem without having to use curly brackets, though.

Being able to control loops via a counter-variable or iterating over all elements of a group of elements frequently does not give us enough control over the data we want to process, so often we also need to provide additional conditions to control our processing actions. We will find out about some of these in the next section, and will keep on practising using them – as well as various types of for loops – again and again when we write larger and more challenging programs.

3.3 MORE REPETITIVENESS (FURTHER LOOPS)

As we have seen in the previous section, for and foreach loops give us a fairly good degree of control over a known range of data, but what if we cannot actually establish the amount/length of data to process beforehand? In this case, we need to make recourse to further types of loops which test 'non-numerical' conditions.

3.3.1 THE *WHILE* LOOP

Perhaps the most important loop of this type is the while loop, which runs for as long as a given condition evaluates to true. One of the most common uses of this is to test and see whether a file contains further lines and, if so, to iterate over them. We will see how to do this in a later section when we discuss *file handling*. Unlike the pseudo-interactive program we wrote earlier to exemplify the unless statement, this one – which we will call 'while_loop.pl' – is truly interactive and will always keep on running until the user types in the word *finish*, in the meantime repeatedly prompting the user to input another word.

```
1  print "Please type in a word and press enter:\nTo
   exit the program, type 'finish'.\n\n";
2  $word = <STDIN>;
3  chomp $word;
4  while ($word ne "finish") {
5    print "\nThe word you typed is '$word'.\n\n";
6    print "Please type in another word and press
     enter:\n\n";
```

```
 7    $word = <STDIN>;
 8    chomp $word;
 9  }
10  print "Program finished.";
```

The first line here is used to prompt the user to provide some input. Previously, we mainly used to react to something that occurred in our programs when we printed out some message, but this time we actually want to engage the user, as in a test. The main instruction is given on the first line that is printed, the additional option on how to exit the program on a second line, while whatever output the program is going to produce will appear two lines below the last instruction in the prompt. The double newline here simply makes it easier for the user to distinguish the original prompt from the output than if we were using a single newline. In the absence of any other formatting options on the command line, separating prompts and output in this way is perhaps one of the best alternatives, although we could also make use of indentation by using leading tabs (\t) or highlighting the output results by adding special markings, such as surrounding double or triple angled brackets (>>> result <<<), to them.

The second and third lines are responsible for retrieving data from the command line and storing it in an appropriate format in $word. In line 2, we use the *line input operator* (also known as the *diamond* operator because of its shape) to retrieve the user input from the command line (STDIN). We will learn more about STDIN and its significance later when we discuss *filehandles*; for now, let us simply equate it with the command line to simplify matters. The diamond operator in this case reads in a line from the command line as soon as the user presses enter, so technically one could provide more than one word of input here. The line that is read in, however, contains not only the text typed on it but also a trailing line break (\n). This is removed from $word by using the chomp function which will be discussed further in the next section.

The while loop from lines 4 to 9 is executed for as long as the condition $word ne "finish" evaluates to true. In other words, our condition controlling the loop applies for as long as our input word is not the word *finish*. This being true, we then first print the content of $word, together with an appropriate message, to the command line (line 5), and prompt the user for another word (line 6). Strictly speaking, we do not actually need to print out this message because we can see the word we typed, anyway, but printing it out here can again be seen as a verification of the input. For example, if we had omitted the chomp operation from line 3, we could immediately see an additional newline in our output here and know that we had made a mistake. Do not test this out yet, though, until you have read to the end of the following paragraph, as otherwise you may be in for a surprise! If, alternatively, the very first word we typed were the word *finish*, the while loop would never be executed at all and we would jump straight to line 10.

On lines 7 and 8, we repeat the operations from lines 2 and 3 to read new input from the command line again. It is important to note that if we did not repeat these operations here, we would never even allow the user to exit the program by typing *finish* because the word contained in $word would always remain the same. In other words, unless the user had typed *finish* in the first place right after starting the program (and the loop would therefore never even start), our program would get stuck in an **endless** loop. Now, this would be a serious problem for us because the program would simply keep on running without any elegant way of interrupting it, but luckily there is a way out of this and you can usually force the interruption of your program by pressing Ctrl + C. The following box contains a syntax summary for the while loop.

```
while (condition) {
  statement(s);
}
```

3.3.2 THE *UNTIL* LOOP

The until loop is the exact counterpart of the while loop, only that, rather than testing whether a condition *is* true, we wait for it to *become* true. Below is the equivalent version of the previous program:

```
1  print "Please type in a word and press enter:\nTo
   exit the program, type 'finish'.\n\n";
2  $word = <STDIN>;
3  chomp $word;
4  until ($word eq "finish") {
5      print "\nThe word you typed is '$word'.\n\n";
6      print "Please type in another word and press
       enter:\n\n";
7      $word = <STDIN>;
8      chomp $word;
9  }
```

Please note that, in order to be able to change the loop from a while to an until one, we also had to reverse the testing condition from ne to eq. Otherwise, our program would terminate on any word but *finish*! The following box contains a syntax summary for the until loop.

```
until (condition) {
  statement(s);
}
```

3.3.3 CONTROLLING LOOPS FURTHER

In the previous example programs, you may have noticed that we had to retrieve the words from the command line in two separate places, once outside the loop and (repeatedly) inside it if the condition was appropriate for continuing. This seems like a bit of redundancy, though, so we would really like to be able to do the retrieving only once and then decide inside the loop whether we want to continue prompting the user or not. Controlling measures like this can be taken by using additional control operators inside loops. We will discuss two of these, `last` and `next`, now, together with some appropriate examples.

Let us start with `last`, as this is most appropriate for controlling the `while` loop example we discussed above and thereby shortening the program. Before we discuss the following version of our `while` loop program, which we will call 'while_loop_short.pl', spend a few minutes to see whether you can already understand what is going on here.

```
1  print "Please type in a word and press enter:\nTo
     exit the program, type 'finish'.\n\n";
2  while ($word = <STDIN>) {
3    chomp $word;
4    last if ($word eq 'finish');
5    print "\nThe word you typed is '$word'.\n\n";
6    print "Please type in another word and press
       enter:\n\n";
7  }
8  print "Program finished.";
```

Line 1 of our program simply stays the same because we still need to keep on prompting the user to type in any word in the first place, but you will probably have noticed that we have dropped the two lines before the loop where we initially retrieved the first word and removed the end-of-line character from it. This task, which will generally be done repeatedly, anyway, is now done inside the loop condition. How this works may be a bit difficult to understand at first, but remember that the basic idea behind specifying a condition is that it has to be something that evaluates to either true or false. Now, as a successful assignment operation is something that evaluates to true, we can exploit this feature and run the loop for as long as we can successfully retrieve a word from the command line. Please note, though, that since our program will now constantly be waiting for input from the command line, we have effectively set up an endless loop again, so that we now need to provide a condition to 'bail out of' this loop again, but this time inside the loop, rather than inside the controlling condition.

This is exactly what we do in line 4, where we use the `last` operator to end the loop if the word the user typed is *finish*. The way we express this condition, however, is also something special because, instead of writing the condition first and then adding the command inside the curly brackets as we have always done before, we now (post)*modify* the command by attaching the condition under which it applies at the end. This is effectively like a *defining relative clause* in English, which also singles out a particular referent by narrowing down the list of its properties and thereby making it easier to pick out exactly who or what we are talking about. Alternatively, of course, we could also see this structure as a form of *focusing* or *clefting*, where the most important part of our statement is expressed first. As so often in language, those are simply two different perspectives on the same thing and you should choose the one for yourself that best helps you to remember this special feature of Perl.

Let us now see how we can use the next operator to control what happens inside a (while) loop. In order to demonstrate this, we will take a look at a slightly modified version of part of our earlier 'extract_nth_element.pl' program, the one where we originally removed the spaces, only that this time we will use a different test string and remove punctuation instead.

```
 1  $string = "This is a test string. We will use this
    for demonstrating how to remove punctuation. Just
    wait and see what happens!";
 2  print "test string: ",$string,"\n";
 3  # split the string into its individual characters
 4  @original_array = split //, $string;
 5  @array_wo_punctuation = ();
 6  # remove punctuation the inefficient way
 7  while ($char = shift (@original_array)) {
 8      next if ($char eq '.' or $char eq '!' or $char
        eq ',');
 9      push @array_wo_punctuation, $char;
10  }
11  print join('', @array_wo_punctuation),"\n";
```

As you can see, our test string in line 1 has been modified to include some punctuation to strip out, but we still print it out for reference in line 2. We also still split the test string into individual characters and store it in an array as before. The array that is set up in line 5, though, has been named more appropriately to indicate that the modified one should not contain any punctuation later.

In lines 7–10, we now use a while loop instead of the foreach loop we employed in the earlier extraction program. As in the shortened while loop example above, we again use an assignment operation as our loop condition, this time removing an element from the beginning of the original array each time we go through the loop and assigning it to the variable $char. Two things are important to note in this context: (1) that we are effectively 'destroying' – well, at least emptying – the original array; and (2) that this time the loop automatically ends once there are no longer any elements left inside the array that could be shifted off.

Inside the loop, we skip over any punctuation marks using the next operator. This operator simply interrupts the loop at the current point and continues testing the loop condition defined at the top of the loop, so that line 9 is never even executed if the modifying if clause evaluates to true. The manner in which we have defined our condition here also demonstrates a new feature, namely that of complex conditions. So far, apart from the assignment operations, we have generally specified single comparison operations as the basis for our conditions, but in this case we actually specify multiple alternatives, and if either one of those is met, then we execute the next statement. Again, this is not the most efficient way of doing this in Perl, but we will not find out about how to do this 'properly' until later, when we introduce regular expressions.

Finally, to round off our program, we print a stringified representation of the joined array, this time specifying an empty 'joiner' because we still retain all our spaces inside the array. As an additional little exercise, think about whether we would really need to use join here at all...

4

WORKING WITH TEXT
(BASIC STRING HANDLING)

4.1 CHOMPING AND CHOPPING

In the previous section, we have already seen one string handling function, the chomp function, which removes a (potential) final newline character from a string. When you use this function, make sure that you do not accidentally confuse it with a function that has a similar name, but completely different functionality, called chop. This function in fact removes any final character whatsoever from a string and returns that character only, instead of the shortened string, so if you use it in an assignment where you intend to actually copy the remainder to the original variable, you will overwrite the original variable with the final character only!

In order to test and help us better understand this behaviour, let us take a look at a short sample program called 'chop_string.pl'.

```
1   $to_chomp = "chomped\n";
2   print "testing the chomp function...\n";
3   print "\$to_chomp before chomping the first time:
    >>>",$to_chomp,"<<<\n";
4   $chomped = chomp $to_chomp;
5   print "the result of the first chomping operation is
    >>>$chomped<<<","\n";
6   print "\$to_chomp is now: >>>", $to_chomp, "<<<\n";
7   print "\$to_chomp before chomping the second time:
    >>>",$to_chomp,"<<<\n";
8   $chomped = chomp $to_chomp;
9   print "the result of the second chomping operation is
    >>>$chomped<<<","\n";
10  print "\$to_chomp is now: >>>", $to_chomp, "<<<\n\n";
11  $to_chop = "chopped\n";
12  print "testing the chop function...\n";
13  print "\$to_chop before chopping the first time: >>>",
    $to_chop, "<<<\n";
14  $chopped = chop $to_chop;
15  print "the result of the first chopping operation is
    >>>$chopped<<<", "\n";
```

48

```
16  print "\$to_chop is now: >>>", $to_chop, "<<<\n";
17  print "\$to_chop before chopping the second time: >>>",
    $to_chop, "<<<\n";
18  $chopped = chop $to_chop;
19  print "the result of the second chopping operation is
    >>>$chopped<<<", "\n";
20  print "\$to_chop is now: >>>", $to_chop, "<<<";
```

The output from this program is shown below:

```
testing the chomp function...
$to_chomp before chomping the first time: >>>chomped <<<
the result of the first chomping operation is >>>1<<<
$to_chomp is now: >>>chomped<<<
$to_chomp before chomping the second time: >>>chomped<<<
the result of the second chomping operation is >>>0<<<
$to_chomp is now: >>>chomped<<<
testing the chop function...
$to_chop before chopping the first time: >>>chopped <<<
the result of the first chopping operation is >>> <<<
$to_chop is now: >>>chopped<<<
$to_chop before chopping the second time: >>>chopped<<<
the result of the second chopping operation is >>>d<<<
$to_chop is now: >>>choppe<<<
```

There should be nothing particularly mysterious about the output of this program apart from maybe the result of the first chomping operation being a *1*, and the second one a *0*. The two variables $to_chomp and $to_chop both initially hold the same string values that end in a newline. The two corresponding variables $chomped and $chopped are used to store and print the results of the chomp and chop operations, respectively.

We carry out the same operation on both variables twice. The result of the first chomping operation shows that the newline string has successfully been removed from $to_chomp. The 1 that is returned by the chomp function actually indicates the same thing and is simply the numerical equivalent of true. The reason why the second chomping operation returns a 0 – the equivalent of false – is that there is no longer a newline to remove inside the variable $to_chomp, so that this variable cannot be changed any longer.

In contrast, the result of the first chopping operation shows that the newline at the end of the original string has been cut off and stored in the variable $chopped. The second time we use the same function, the final letter of the remaining string is removed and the result again stored in $chopped. Each time the function is used, a final character is removed until there are no characters left, in which case an empty string will be returned.

So far, we have always assumed that one newline is always the same as another because, in Perl, it is always internally represented as \n. This may seem true to you if you only ever work on one platform – or at least you will never notice any problems then. However, if you want your Perl programs to be able to run on different operating systems, you need to be aware of the fact that different operating systems use different conventions for representing line breaks. Thus, DOS/Windows-based systems in fact use two characters (\r\l, or CRLF) for text files, a carriage return (\r; ASCII name CR, character number 13; octal \015) plus a line feed (\l; ASCII name: LF, character number: 10; octal \012), Unix/Linux systems only the linefeed (\l), and older Mac systems only use the carriage return.

This may lead to problems, for example when you read in data from text files under Linux that were created on a Windows computer, in which case the chomp function will happily remove the line feed (\l), but leave a trailing carriage return (\r) at the end of each line. Now, imagine that you might then process that data, splitting the line into a word and its associated part-of-speech (PoS) tag, putting each key-value pair into a hash representing a dictionary. In the next step of your program, you might then have a list of words extracted from a sentence and want to look up the word in the dictionary to identify its PoS. Let us assume then that you want to extract a list of all nouns from the sentence, so you check to see whether the key in the hash has an N (for noun) tag associated with it, using the eq operator of course. However, this will fail each time, simply because the value that is stored in the hash is never going to be an *N* for nouns, but an *N*\r instead, as the trailing carriage return has never been removed from the line end. Do not worry too much about this, though, as we will soon learn about ways of fixing this kind of problem.

4.2 EXTRACTING A SUBSTRING FROM A LONGER STRING

In order to achieve what we may not be able to do by using the chop function, we can use the substr function, which allows us to extract a part (*substring*) of a string, at the same time leaving the original string intact. Let us see how this is done by looking at a slightly longer program, which you should type into your editor and save as 'verbform_tester.pl':

```
1   $verbform = shift;
2   $form = "";
3   $base = "";
4   if (substr($verbform, -1) eq "s") {
5     $form = " 3rd person singular";
6     $base = substr $verbform, 0, -1;
7   }
8   elsif(substr($verbform, -2) eq "ed") {
9     $form = " a past participle or past tense form";
10    $base = substr $verbform, 0, -2;
11  }
12  elsif (substr($verbform, -3) eq "ing") {
13    $form = " an ing form";
```

```
14    $base = substr $verbform, 0, -3;
15  }
16  else {
17    $form = " an infinitive or non-3rd person
      singular form";
18    $base = $verbform;
19  }
20  print "The verbform is $form and its base is
      '$base'.";
```

In the above program, we can even see two different forms of using the substr function, one with two (lines 4, 8, 12) and one with three arguments (lines 6, 10, 14). The first argument always has to be a string or string variable. The second argument specifies the starting offset and the third one the end offset. If no end offset is specified, as in lines 4, 8 and 12 in our example, the function returns everything from the start offset to the end of the string. Just as with arrays, the first position/offset in the string is 0 (see lines 6, 10, 14). Negative offsets, as can be seen in all examples of the function above, refer to offsets to the left from the end of the string, for example, in line 4 the last character of the string/word (substr ($verbform, -1)). If you have paid close attention to the code above, you may also have noticed that I used the substr function in two slightly different ways with regard to brackets around the arguments. As a minor exercise, try to come up with an explanation for this, but if you should not manage to do so, this will be explained a little further below in section 4.5.

As you can clearly see, the substr function is ideally suited to conducting simple morphological analyses, although at closer inspection our program turns out to be less than perfect. To help you understand it a little better, I will give a brief summary here.

In lines 1–3, we first retrieve a command line argument, store it in the variable $verbform, and then declare and initialise two further variables, $form and $base, to empty strings. Within the if or elsif conditions in lines 4, 8 and 12, we extract strings of length 1–3 characters respectively, and compare them to the strings that make up the suffixes {-s}, {-ed} and {-ing}. If any one of these conditions holds true, we store an appropriate comment as to the type of inflection/word class in the variable $form and store the base form of the verb in $base by extracting the substring, starting with the first letter of the verb, and up to the start of the suffix.

If none of the earlier conditions apply, we can assume that we are left either with a bare infinitive or any other non-third person singular form, in which case the base is equal to the whole verbform. Once we have tested all the conditions and filled the variables appropriately, we can now output a message detailing which type of inflectional form we have identified and what the base would be.

As a little exercise to hone your linguistic analysis skills and algorithmic thinking, try to identify cases/types of verbs where our program may go wrong in its 'interpretation'. You should definitely be able to find a few and explain why this may be the case. Also think about whether you could suggest ways of improving it.

4.3 'ADDING' STRINGS TOGETHER

Putting multiple strings (or string variables) together to create a longer string is referred to as *concatenation*. Concatenating strings is achieved by putting a dot (.) between them. For example, rather than interpolating the variables $form and $base into the message string in line 20 above, we could have written the print instruction like this, making it a little clearer that we are using two variables in our output: print "The verbform is ".$form." and its base is '".$base."'.";. One very important thing to remember when 'adding' strings together, though, is not to forget any potential spaces in the strings around the variables because otherwise you may end up with rather strange new 'compounds'.

My reference to compounds above should already have given you a clue as to which area of linguistics concatenation may be most relevant. One of its most obvious uses can be found in the generation of morphological variants of words, maybe for testing hypotheses about morphological processes or language generation in *expert, dialogue*, or *Q & A* (question and answer) *systems* that provide a verbal output for their users, as well as many other related uses. In order to investigate this further, let us do a couple of exercises again.

[**Exercise 8**] The first one of these exercises is to improve the generation of ordinal numbers from our 'extract_nth_element.pl' program (p. 39) by eliminating the curly brackets around the variable identifier that we had to use in the interpolation process. Remember that, there, we had to use constructions like $ordinal = "${n}st"; in order to interpolate $n into a string that we then in turn assigned to the 'auxiliary' variable $ordinal. However, if we had actually known how to concatenate the appropriate ordinal suffix to $n, we could have saved ourselves the effort of typing the curly brackets. Furthermore, since we were not really going to need the cardinal value of $n again, we could have simply made do without the variable $ordinal in the first place by modifying $n through concatenating it with the appropriate ending inside the if-elsif-else construction, and then assigning the result back to $n. In order to practise this:

1. Copy the original version of the program to another program called 'extract_nth_element_concat.pl'.
2. Modify the program to eliminate the variable $ordinal and change the interpolation of $n to a form that uses concatenation instead.
3. Do not forget to modify the final statement appropriately, too!

[**Exercise 9**] As a further exercise, we will now write a program, called 'test_prefixation.pl', which will allow us to see whether a number of words given as command line arguments can be used with a particular prefix. Inside the program,

1. First retrieve/remove the prefix from the arguments array and store it in $prefix.
2. Copy the remainder of the arguments from @ARGV to a new array called @bases.

3. Use an appropriate loop to iterate over all the elements in the array,
4. prefixing each element in turn and printing out the resulting form for verification on the command line.
5. Test the program using the following lists of prefixes and words:
    prefix: {in}; words: *edible, possible, suitable, capable, legible*
    prefix: {re}; words: *apply, read, follow, do, see, think, remain*
    prefix: {non-}; words: *man, sense, human, car, word.*

In case you still have difficulties in understanding how to get the right number of arguments off the command line into the appropriate variables, take a look at Table 4.1 that shows what happens when we apply the `shift` operator to @ARGV as opposed to retrieving arguments by copying them. We will use the example of the prefix {in} from above:

Table 4.1   An illustration of the difference between shifting and copying from an array

	$prefix	@ARGV[0]	@ARGV[1]	@ARGV[2]	@ARGV[3]
before shifting		in	edible	possible	suitable
after shifting	in	edible	possible	suitable	capable
before copying		in	edible	possible	suitable
after copying	in	in	edible	possible	suitable

As you can see quite clearly, when using the `shift` operator, removing the first element form @ARGV makes it possible for us to simply copy the remainder of @ARGV into @bases without having to think about how many elements are left in it. If, in contrast, we copied the first element out of @ARGV, we would then first have to establish the overall number of arguments – in other words, the length of the complete arguments array – and then use a `for` loop that starts at position 1 and runs until it reaches the end of the array, appending each element to @bases in turn to copy them. The copying approach therefore works fairly well if we have a small and fixed number of arguments only, whereas the `shift` approach is best used when a fixed number of required arguments is followed by a potentially variable number of additional ones.

This exercise could easily be used to set up a test scenario for language learners, to verify the acceptability of prefix-base combinations, or to illustrate phonological conditioning in word formation. As an optional exercise, you could rewrite the above program to accept and produce suffigated word forms, for instance to simulate the verb forms that could be tested with the verbform tester.

4.4 ESTABLISHING THE LENGTH OF A STRING

Sometimes, when we do linguistic research, it is important to be able to measure the length of words. For example, if we plan to investigate issues of morphological complexity, such as words that have been created by adding multiple affixes, it really does not even begin to make sense to start looking at any words that are shorter than maybe 8 to 10 characters minimally. Conversely, since the investigation of swear words is no longer a taboo, we may want to be able to extract all four- or five-letter words from a large corpus of everyday language to investigate how many or which ones of them are indeed swear words, as the expression 'four-letter-word' may lead us to believe.

[**Exercise 10**] Establishing the `length` of a string (in characters) is quite simple, as we can use the equally named function. Since we still do not know how to read in lots of words from a file as a basis for an extended analysis, let us test this by doing another contrived exercise that combines concatenating and 'measuring' the length of some strings we feed it. We will call this program 'test_length.pl'.

1. Using the `shift` operator, retrieve two string arguments from the command line and store them in the variables `$str1` and `$str2`.
2. Set up another string variable `$final_string` to later hold the result of the concatenation operation and initialise it to an empty string.
3. Set up three numerical variables `$length1`, `$length2` and `$final_length` and initialise them to 0 each. These will be used to record the length of the different strings.
4. Next, with both `$str1` and `$str2` as arguments, use the `length` function and assign the results to `$length1` and `$length2` respectively.
5. Also print out a message that contains the value of each string and its length.
6. Concatenate `$str1` and `$str2`, adding a space in between the two, and assign the result to `$final_string`.
7. Establish the length of `$final_string` and assign it to `$final_length`.
8. Print out a message that contains information about the final string, its length and its component strings.

As I said before, this exercise is not really very useful for anything but to give you practice in trying to get used to the two operations of concatenating and establishing the length of strings, apart from allowing you to consolidate your knowledge from previous sections. However, from now on, I promise that we will start doing more practical and useful exercises again.

4.5 HANDLING CASE

We have previously learnt that computers do make a distinction between what we normally refer to as small and capital letters, which are more correctly referred to as *lowercase* and *uppercase characters* in computing terms. In our first examples of simulating syntactic inversion, we simply chose to ignore the fact that sentence-initial words are normally capitalised but of course, if we want to be able to generate orthographically correct sentences, then we should definitely try to fix the output after the inversion. [**Exercise 11**] To practise this, we will write a short program called 'sentence_case.pl' but, before we start, we still need to discuss two things that will help us to make this program work and to do so in an efficient way.

The first thing we need to know is that we can use the `ucfirst` function to ensure that the first character of a string will be uppercased. The other thing is something to do with how we use functions, especially how the arguments to them may be presented inside the program. You may not really have been properly aware of this, although I tried to make you aware of this in section 4.2, but we have already used Perl's built-in functions in two different 'ways', one where the comma-separated list of arguments was simply added after the function name (cf. the `print` function), and the other (cf. the `substr` function in 'verbform_tester.pl') where the arguments were enclosed in round brackets. The best practice recommendation made in Conway (2005: 13) is to avoid using the round brackets for all built-in functions, although it may sometimes be necessary to use them to make it easier to see which arguments belong to which functions. This is especially important if you chain the functions, using the result of one function as the argument to another, something that helps us to make our code more compact and to avoid having to use intermediate/temporary variables. In this case, Conway recommends to attach the brackets to the function name without any intervening space to distinguish them visually from operators, such as `if`, that are followed by conditions or similar control constructs in round brackets. In designing our program, we want to take advantage of this 'chaining' feature by using the result of the `join` function as the argument to the `ucfirst` function to capitalise our sentence that we produce from an array of words.

1. Set up an array of words and initialise it to the three words *they,* *are* and *linguists.*
2. Print out a string with three arguments, a 'before' message to indicate the sentence state before we manipulate the array, the joined array with uppercased first letter and finally a full stop and newline.
3. Next, swap the first two elements of @words, using list context instead of a temporary variable.
4. Finally, print out another message that indicates the 'after' state, this time with a question mark as the third argument.

The counterpart to the `ucfirst` function we used above is the `lcfirst` function, which we could, for instance, use if we wanted to ensure that we treat all word forms that occur in sentence-initial position like their potential lowercase equivalents, for example, for counting the frequencies of all word forms (cf. section 9.2), although this would of course also affect sentence-initial proper nouns or acronyms, so we should be somewhat careful when doing this or at least be aware of the potential problems such an approach might cause. Now, if you wanted to ensure that all your data in a string is in either uppercase or lowercase, you could use the `uc` (uppercase) and the `lc` (lowercase) function respectively. Such an approach is frequently taken in constructing alphabetically sorted word lists (cf. section 8.2), such as for dictionaries, where you would want to sort both upper- and lowercase words together under the same initial letter.

5

WORKING WITH STORED DATA
(BASIC FILE HANDLING)

As we have already seen in some of the previous sections, often simple strings that we type in ourselves or that we prompt a user to provide do not really represent an interesting or valid way of obtaining materials to prove or disprove our linguistic hypotheses. For most purposes, we need to be able to process a sufficiently large amount of data before we can make any claims at all. And even if we only need a limited amount of data for testing purposes, such as a few words or phrases, it may sometimes be too cumbersome to have to type these on the command line repeatedly, for example, if we want to refine our programs and keep on testing them on the same data over and over again. For larger programs, it may also be necessary to store dictionaries or configuration files and so on, on disk, in order to read them in every time the program starts.

For these and other purposes, we need to be able to interact with our operating system to access and manipulate these files in a way that goes beyond the simple command line redirection we used earlier to store our output from 'base_charset.pl' in a text file. In this section, we will investigate how to achieve such an interaction in a way that is also appropriate for dealing with texts in today's multilingual society. Furthermore, since file and directory handling are very similar in nature, and in fact often go hand-in-hand, we will also discuss the latter in this chapter.

When we want to work with files stored on a hard disk or other medium, we not only need to be able to specify an absolute or relative path to the file we want to work with, but also to provide a way of *referencing* the file. This is achieved by assigning a *filehandle* to each file we want to process, no matter whether we want to open it for *reading*, *writing*, *appending to* or *modifying* (editing) it. Let us now learn how to do this, beginning with a look into how to open files.

5.1 OPENING A FILEHANDLE

Opening a filehandle is achieved via the aptly named `open` function. This function, at least in the form that we will learn to use it on this course, usually takes the name of the filehandle, a *mode* for opening the handle and a file name as arguments. The last two can also be combined into one string, but I would actually advise against using this technique, as it will effectively prevent us from employing some useful tricks to deal with data in different character sets later. Thus, if we wanted to be able to process the contents of our very first program ('first_prog.pl'), we could use the open function in this way: `open $IN, "<", "first_prog.pl";`. The left-pointing angled

Table 5.1   Essential file handling modes

mode	operator
read(-only)	<
write(-only)	>
append	>>
read + write	+<

bracket (<) here shows that the mode for input is set to *read-only*. Table 5.1 shows a list of some of the different modes we may use for operations on filehandles, most of which we already introduced briefly in our earlier discussion of redirection.

The name of the filehandle is usually – by convention – given in all-uppercase letters and it is also recommended (Conway 2005: 204) that you prefix each filehandle – apart from obviously the built-in default ones, which we will discuss further below, but generally do not want to mess with – with a $ symbol, just like a scalar variable. This will later also allow us to *localise* them, once we have learnt how to do so in section 10.1.3.

Using the syntax shown above would now enable us to read the contents of the file because it effectively links the file*name* to a file*handle*, at the same time specifying what we are allowed to do with this file. However, we still need to explore how to effectively deal with the file's content in the most sensible way(s). Before we do so, though, we will first take a brief look at how to interrupt our program gracefully in case there happens to be an error in creating the filehandle, that is in accessing the file, in the first place. This type of *error handling* can be implemented by creating a compound statement that specifies an alternative action in case the operation fails, and involves the use of the logical operator or – which we first encountered in our recent exercise (p. 46) where we removed the punctuation from a string – as well as the die function. Thus, a more elegant and fool-proof way of trying to open our filehandle would be: open $IN, "<", "first_prog.pl" or die "unable to open first_prog.pl!\n";.

As its name implies, the die function causes the program to abort, displaying an appropriate error message which is defined by the program's author and provided as its argument(s). The optional plural indication in the previous sentence is deliberate, as the error message can in fact consist of a list that is automatically concatenated. Thus die works like print, only with the additional function of interrupting the program. The newline at the end of the error message in our example above is used to suppress the (potentially less meaningful) error message that would otherwise be generated automatically by the perl interpreter.

Before you start 'messing around' with files, though, a brief, but highly important note concerning (write) access to files is in order: **Whenever you open previously existing files for write access, always bear in mind that they will be recreated as blank files and all their contents will be overwritten, even if your program does not send any output to them!** Thus, always think twice about the way you are going to open a file, unless of course you are pretty sure that you want to recreate the data in a modified way. If you are unsure about whether something may go wrong and you would rather retain the original data until you have ascertained that it is safe to delete, you might want to opt for *non-destructive* processing by either creating a new file to write to or writing the file out to a different directory.

5.2 TWEAKING YOUR INPUT AND/OR OUTPUT OPTIONS

So far, we have usually implicitly accepted that the program files we created would be in whatever the default encoding for files on our computer is. However, the file mode can also further be 'constrained' by adding information about the assumed or intended encoding of the file via Perl's *I/O layers*. Otherwise, the default encoding configured for your computer will just be assumed. Which one exactly this will be depends on which *locale* has been set up on the computer, which in turn usually depends on where you live in the world, unless you know how to manipulate this yourself.

To specify an encoding for input or output, you add a colon, the keyword `encoding` and the name of an encoding – in round brackets – after the redirection symbol, for example, `"<:encoding(utf-8)"`. The preceding example will allow you to read from a file that has been encoded with the variable length Unicode encoding UTF-8, which just so happens to be the encoding that Perl uses internally to represent characters, anyway. And although we will mainly be dealing with English text on this course, it still makes sense to encode all our files as UTF-8 from now on, partly because all the basic characters that occur in English (in the range from 0 to 127) actually occur at the same code points there, but partly also because this still leaves us with the option to include other characters in our files that may not appear in the basic ASCII or Latin1 character ranges. Using Unicode, we can also process phonetic characters, for example, provided that we have managed to get them into a file in the first place or can access/produce them through a GUI.

Being able to specify separate encodings for input and output also allows us to do *file conversion* from one encoding to another, for example if we have some old corpus data in some form of non-Unicode (*legacy*) encoding that we want to be able to process with a multilingual application that expects some form of Unicode input, or simply to ensure future 'portability'.

5.3 READING FROM A FILEHANDLE

Once we have opened a filehandle successfully, there are essentially three different ways of processing the associated file. The first one involves reading all the lines into an array and then iterating over its elements (array context), the second one using a `while` loop to achieve the same thing (scalar context) and the third one to read the whole file into a single, potentially very large, string (another form of scalar context). In general, at least in most cases, the second one is to be preferred because it enables us to save on resources as only one line at a time is physically stored in memory each time we pass through the loop, which is especially important when dealing with very large files.

To read from the filehandle, we need to make use of the *diamond operator* (`<>`) we used earlier for retrieving our user input from the command line while the program was already running. The only difference in the way we use the diamond operator here is that, instead of having nothing (or STDIN) inside the angled brackets, we now write <$IN> instead to refer to the filehandle we opened earlier. Just like variable names, any filehandle identifiers you create can have (almost) arbitrary names that usually ought to reflect their purpose. This is why I picked the name $IN to reflect that we are going to open a file for input, although of course I could have equally well chosen $INPUT or $INPUT_FILE, just that the latter two are longer and only marginally more explicit.

5.3.1 FILE PROCESSING IN LIST CONTEXT

If we now wanted to read in the whole file and store all the lines inside an array named @lines, we could simply write @lines = <$IN>;. We can compare this operation to copying all the elements of one array/list to another if we see the input file simply as a list of lines. Such an approach would be sensible in those cases where the file we are trying to read in is reasonably small, maybe up to a few megabytes in size, so we would certainly have no problem whatsoever reading in any of our programs. Another reason for wanting to process a file as an array of lines might, for example, be if we had an *interlinear* version of some text, where each odd line may contain the original source text and each even one a translation, and we would want to extract and store each language version in a different file. [**Exercise 12**] Let us just test reading in a file and printing its contents out on the command line in a little program called 'file_reading.pl'. Inside this file:

1. Set up a file handle as shown above to read in 'first_prog.pl', also specifying UTF-8 as the input encoding.
2. Make sure that you use the correct redirection symbol and also add some appropriate error handling!
3. Declare an array called @lines and read in all the lines from the filehandle in list context.
4. Set up a counter variable called $line_count and initialise it to 0.
5. Set up an appropriate loop to iterate over all the lines stored in the array.
6. Inside the loop,
   a. first increase the line counter by one,
   b. then print out the current line number, followed by a colon, a tab and finally the line itself.

The output of this program on the command line, as shown below, should be the program text of your 'first_prog.pl' file, but prefixed by line numbers as you might be able to see them in your editor if you have an option for displaying line numbers there.

```
1:  #!/usr/bin/perl
2:  print "This is a book on programming Perl.\n";
3:  print "You are currently reading the chapter on
        \"Basic Programming Concepts.\"\n";
```

In the instructions, I deliberately left the choice of a loop to iterate over the lines up to you, simply because, as we have already learnt, TMTOWTDI. One option would be to use a `while` loop, shifting off each line in turn as we did in the modified version of 'extract_nth_element.pl' and printing it, together with the counter. Another one would be a counter-driven `for` loop that runs from 0 to the last index position of the array, in which case we would not necessarily need `$line_count`, either, because each current line number inside the loop would simply be the current index position + 1. This, however, would not be an optimal solution if we wanted to create a 'clean' copy of our file, for example, without comments or empty lines by skipping over them. This is why I would personally opt for a `foreach` loop where we could first check to see whether we would want to skip a line based on specific criteria using `next`, or otherwise increase the line counter and print the information.

There is still one small 'problem' with this program, though. Once we have finished accessing the file in question, we really ought to close (release) the filehandle again. This is achieved by using the `close` function with the name of the filehandle as its argument. Please note that, although all filehandles are automatically closed when your program finishes, you should still close them explicitly whenever possible. This enables you to avoid any side effects if you should ever modify and/or enlarge your programs later and thereby potentially create the risk of accidentally overwriting data. For good measure, you should now add an appropriate statement to your version of the above program.

5.3.2 FILE PROCESSING IN LINE CONTEXT

To loop over all the lines in the file in a scalar context, we use a `while` loop whose condition is simply the filehandle inside the diamond operator, thus `while (<$IN>) {...}`. This 'shorthand' expression should be read as "while there are still lines left in the file the handle refers to, retrieve them one at a time". This is because the diamond operator only returns a *single* line each time it is 'called upon' in a scalar context. This may in fact prove a potential source of error if used inappropriately, for instance, when one uses a scalar variable as the left-hand side expression and expecting to read the whole file into a string (in analogy to the array/list context), as in `$lines = <$IN>;`, while in reality only the first line of the file is retrieved.

When processing each line in turn in either of the two contexts discussed so far, we still need to bear in mind that normally each of these lines will actually contain a *trailing* newline character, which we may need to `chomp`, depending on what kind of processing we want to perform on the line. If you are iterating over an array of lines, there is no need to do this chomping inside a loop, though, as this function can equally well be applied to the whole array and not only a single scalar. We also need to remember that when we use the syntax introduced for the `while` loop above (or a `foreach` loop, for that matter), each line that is retrieved will end up in the default variable `$_`, unless we explicitly store it in a different variable. To store the line in a different variable, you simply do an assignment inside the round brackets like this: `while ($line = <$IN>) {...}`. This works because a successful assignment to the variable returns true, just like retrieving a line via the filehandle would. [**Exercise 13**] Test this by writing a modified version of 'file_reading.pl', called 'loop_file_reading.pl', alternately trying out the variant using the default variable and the one where you do an explicit assignment.

5.3.3 SLURPING IN SCALAR CONTEXT

The third option for getting data from a file is idiomatically referred to as *slurping* and involves reading the whole file into a scalar variable. Now normally, as we saw above, accessing a filehandle in scalar context only returns a single line at a time, so we have to use a little trick to achieve our goal. This trick is to set the *input record separator* $/, which normally defaults to \n, to an undefined value: $/ = undef;. This, however, is only safe if you are either only reading in a single file or if you immediately reset $/ to its regular value after having read in the file – otherwise this may well affect your processing of any later files that you did not want to slurp in! Slurping may be a useful way of dealing with files that you do not need to process in a line-based fashion, for example if you only want to do global *replace* operations, maybe updating copyright information in a file or expanding abbreviations and so forth. We will soon learn about how to do global replacements of this type once we have covered the topic of *substitution*.

Being able to change $/ in this way also has some other useful functions. For example, if you want to read in a file in paragraph mode, you can set it to an empty string ($/ = "";) and perl will treat all sequences of text that are separated by two or more newlines as single units, retrieving them from the file one at a time. As a matter of fact, you could potentially set $/ to any specific string you want, so you technically have the option to split a text (naively) at each declarative sentence boundary by setting it to " . ", a full stop followed by a space. However, you may then be in for a few surprises if your text should contain any abbreviations...

5.4 DEFAULT FILEHANDLES

Before we discuss filehandles that you may be creating and opening yourself for writing to, we first ought to spend some time on clarifying the notion of *default filehandles*. Just like the default variable $_ we encountered again above, which will always contain the current element in a list or loop context, we also have some filehandles that are automatically opened when your program starts. These are STDIN (for input; usually the command line), STDOUT (for displaying output; usually the command line), and STDERR (for printing error messages; usually the command line as well). Although the last two usually use the same screen device for output, they are in fact distinct from each other, and technically all three default filehandles can also be redirected.

The fact that these three handles are always opened without the user first having to do this explicitly also accounts for why we have been able to read input from STDIN or print messages to STDOUT previously. Without this, our programs would have never accepted any input nor shown any output or error messages! Please note, too, that these *global* filehandles should not be prefixed by a $ sign like the ones we saw above, as otherwise you would actually be creating new filehandles, rather than using the built-in ones, and perl would obviously not understand that you intend to use the defaults.

5.5 WRITING TO A FILEHANDLE

Writing to a file is essentially a simple matter because, rather than sending your output to STDOUT via the print function, you simply 'redirect' it to your filehandle, only without any redirection symbol. The only thing to observe when you do this is that, although the filehandle in this case is passed to the function as its first argument before any string, it should not be separated from the string arguments by a comma, but only a space. However, the interpreter should normally throw an error message if you mistakenly add the comma, anyway, so you would soon know about your mistake. Printing the contents of a variable $line to a filehandle $OUT would therefore require the following statement: print $OUT $line;. [**Exercise 14**] Let us practise this by writing a little program that copies the contents of one file to another and which we will therefore just call 'file_copy.pl'.

1. Declare two variables $in_file and $out_file to hold the file names and initialise them by retrieving the first two command line arguments.
2. Open a filehandle $IN for the input file in read-only mode. Do not forget the error handling we discussed above!
3. Open a filehandle $OUT for the output file in write mode.
4. Loop over $IN and write each line to $OUT.
5. Close both filehandles.
6. Add some print statements that provide appropriate feedback to the user as to which stage the program is currently in, as well as which files are being read or written to.

Of course, it should not be difficult to see how we could turn this program into a program that converts files from one encoding to another by specifying two different encodings for in- and output, for example to turn a file previously encoded in Latin1 or some other legacy code page to UTF-8, something I have found myself doing quite frequently in order to be able to handle data from different languages in a uniform and consistent way. If you want to do an additional exercise, you can create a new version of the above program that allows you to specify both input and output encoding on the command line alongside the filenames, which will give you a useful file encoding converter.

5.6 WORKING WITH DIRECTORIES

Accessing directories is fairly similar to accessing files. Instead of using a filehandle, though, we now use a *directory handle* with the opendir command instead. Thus, the statement opendir $DIR, "."; would give us a handle on the current directory. We can then use this handle to produce a list of all the files stored in the directory by using the readdir function in list context to store all the file names in an array. Do not accidentally use it in scalar context, as this will only return the name of whatever the next file in the directory is, just like the filehandle only returned a single line in scalar context. To close the directory handle again, use the closedir function with the name of the directory handle as an argument, closedir $DIR; in our case.

Once we have the list of files in an array, we can produce a listing similar to the dir or ls commands of the operating systems that we learnt about in the section that introduced you to the command line. Having a list of all the files in a directory also allows us to process them all in turn, but in most cases we would first want to filter them for specific file types, which is something we will be able to do once we have learnt about *regular expressions* and the grep operator later. [**Exercise 15**] For now, we will just contend ourselves by writing a short program called 'dir_reading.pl', which will output a directory listing. In this file:

1. Retrieve a directory name from the command line and store it in the variable $dir_name.
2. Declare an array to store the file names in later.
3. Open a directory handle $DIR for the directory.
4. Use readdir to store all the filenames in the file list array.
5. Close the directory handle again.
6. Use a foreach loop to print out all the file names inside the array in form of a directory listing.
7. Test the program with a few different absolute and relative path names. On Windows, remember to replace the path separator by a forward slash instead of the backslash to avoid unnecessary side effects because of the backslash being interpreted as an escape symbol.

When you printed out the list of files from the array, you hopefully noticed that the result was a list of bare filenames, without any directory information included. Having the file names in this form is often not very useful, though, because we generally need a *fully qualified* path to the files we want to process, at least if we are not only processing files in the directory our program was called from. In order to process the individual files, we therefore need to prepend the appropriate path information to the file name, which we could either do in a foreach loop or using Perl's highly useful map function. The latter allows us to transform a list of elements into another list (or even a hash) by specifying a block (or function) containing the modification instructions as the first argument, and the list that is to be transformed as the second. Assuming that there is no trailing slash at the end of our path name, which we would otherwise need to remove first, and our array is imaginatively called @files, we could turn our bare list of filenames into one that contains the directory information + filename by saying @files_with_dir = map {$dir_name.'/'.$_} @files;.

Of course, if we had never needed the file list without the directory information in the first place, we could have even created our list of files with fully qualified path names by transforming the results of the readdir function, which – as we know

– returns a list, into an appropriate array directly, as in `@files_with_dir =
map {$dir_name.'/'.$_} readdir $DIR;`, saving ourselves one array
variable. The only real problem with this approach might be that if we did not filter
out the . and .. files that will automatically be included in the file list – or possibly any
other non-text files for that matter – and tried to process all these files, we may get
some error messages related to permission or other file access problems.

Before we can even attempt to deal with at least the first problem (of the . and ..
files), we first ought to learn about a few more functions and features that will allow
us to interact with the operating system to be able to perform *non-destructive* file
processing. **However, I again need to stress here that you need to be very careful
in using some of these functions, so that you will not accidentally destroy some
important and/or valuable data!**

The first of these system-interaction functions we want to discuss here is one that
allows you to create a new directory. It is called `mkdir`, and takes an absolute or
relative path as its first argument. You can optionally also specify the permissions for
the newly created directory as the second argument, but discussing this is beyond the
limits of this course. As you will probably remember, the command name is the same
one that you can also use at the command line on Windows/Linux to achieve this
effect, only that it is much more convenient – and often necessary – to be able to use
it out of your own programs. Just as with opening filehandles and other operations
that occur at system level and may therefore depend on permissions or other issues
that could be beyond your or the program user's control, it is generally also advisable
to use some error handling to ensure that the operation was actually successful, too.
Depending on how important it may be for your program to have a given directory
created for you, you may here either opt for the `die` function we discussed above, or
its more 'lenient' version, `warn`, which will allow the program to continue running
and just emits whatever warning you specify as an argument. [**Exercise 16**] Let us
practise using this function by creating a program called 'make_bk_folder.pl' that will
allow us to set up a backup folder in any (base) directory we might want to specify.

1. Set up a variable called `$base_dir` and initialise it from the command line.
2. Set up a test to see whether the path in `$base_dir` already contains a trailing
   forward slash. If it does not, add one. Hint: `substr` may possibly come in handy
   here...
3. Use the `mkdir` function to set up a folder called 'backup' inside the base directory,
   but do not forget to add some error handling that emits some form of more-or-less
   serious warning in case this should not be possible.
4. Print out an appropriate message to indicate success, provided that the folder can
   be created successfully.
5. Use the program to create the backup folder and manually copy all your programs
   that you have written so far into it.
6. Try to run the program again with the same argument and observe what happens.

When you tried to rerun the program, you should have noted that Perl will not
actually allow you to do this. The really nice thing about this, though, is that, unlike

opening an existing filehandle for write access, trying to create an existing folder does not overwrite its contents...

Obviously, the program we just created above is of limited use because it only allows us to create backup folders, but would it not be nice if we could also use it to specify a source directory to read from and copy all relevant non-system files to the backup folder automatically? As we saw earlier, this is not easily possible without being aware of the fact that we might need to exclude some directories or other files, and dealing with this problem accordingly. Well, in order to determine some of the properties of certain files and to see whether they might be 'worth' copying or not, we can use some of the so-called *file test operators*, possibly in conjunction with their file names. Table 5.2 shows a list of some of those that may be relevant for our purposes.

Table 5.2   Basic file tests

test	function
-e	file exists
-f	file is a plain file (not a directory)
-d	file is a directory

As you can see, each test begins with a hyphen, followed by a single letter. The argument to the test may be either a filename or handle. Let us now take a look at how we could write one version of our revised and extended 'backup' program that illustrates the use of some of these tests and which we will simply call 'backup.pl'.

```
1   # add usage message if less than two arguments have
    been specified
2   die "usage: <name of base_dir> (to create backup
    in) <name of source_dir> (to back up from)!\n" if
    (scalar(@ARGV) < 2);
3   ($base_dir,$source_dir) = (shift,shift);
4   # test if path separator is already present for
    both directories; if not, append it
5   foreach $dir ($base_dir,$source_dir) {
6       if (substr($dir, -1) ne '/') {
7           $dir .= '/' ;
8       }
9   }
10  # test to see whether backup folder exists
11  # if it doesn't...
12  if (!-e $base_dir.'backup') {
13      # try to create it
14      mkdir $base_dir.'backup' or die "unable to
        create backup folder!";
15      # print out a success-indicating message
```

```
16      print "created backup folder in ",
        $base_dir,"\n";
17  }
18  # otherwise ...
19  else {
20      print "backup folder already exists in ",
        $base_dir,"\n";
21  }
22  # get a list of files in the source directory
23  opendir $SOURCE, $source_dir or die "unable to
    read from source directory $source_dir!";
24  @files = readdir $SOURCE;
25  close $SOURCE;
26  # start backing them up in turn...
27  print "beginning backup from $source_dir to backup
    folder in $base_dir ...\n";
28  foreach $file (@files) {
29      # test to see whether the file is not a
        directory
30      if (!-d $source_dir.$file) {
31          # if it is not, open it and write it to new
            file in the backup folder
32          open $IN, "<:encoding(utf-8)", $source_dir
            .$file or warn "unable to open source file
            $file for reading!\n";
33          open $OUT, ">:encoding(utf-8)", $base_dir
            .'backup/'.$file or warn "unable to open
            source file $file for reading!\n";
34          while (<$IN>) {
35                  print $OUT $_;
36          }
37          close $IN; close $OUT;
38      }
39  }
40  print "finished backup.";
```

The above program is certainly not a perfect backup program, but it still demonstrates nicely how we can employ what we have learnt so far about error handling, string handling, directory access, as well as file tests, to deal with at least some of the problems we need to face in designing such a program. I have again tried to make it easier to understand by adding a few comments, and we will also discuss some further details now.

The program begins by checking the @ARGV array to see whether at least two arguments have been provided at startup (line 2) and exits with a usage message in case there are fewer arguments. It does this by establishing the length of @ARGV through the `scalar` operator, whose result is used in the comparison with the < operator. If two or more arguments were specified, we `shift` off the first two and assign them to `$base_dir` – where we want to create the backup folder if it does not already exist – and `$source_dir` (which we are going to get the data to back up from), respectively (line 3).

The next step (lines 4–9) involves some error handling – or rather prevention – because we cannot predict whether the user will in fact specify either of the two path names with or without a trailing path separator. To simplify the matter, as well as to be able to simply append our source and target filenames later to have a fully qualified path to each file, we use the `substr` function to retrieve the final character of each of the two path names inside the `foreach` loop, test to see whether it is a slash, and append one if there is not already one present. In order not to have to rewrite the same test + potential concatenation operation twice, we use a little trick, which consists in setting up a list context for the `foreach` loop instead of an array. The list we process inside the loop takes both the variables for the path names in turn and makes the strings contained inside them accessible via the auxiliary loop variable `$dir`, which is then manipulated inside the loop. In other words, the auxiliary variable here acts like an *alias* for each variable inside the list!

Lines 10–21 are devoted to ensuring that a suitable backup folder exists in the base directory, or to creating one if it doesn't. In line 12, we first use the file test operator -e in conjunction with the negation operator ! to test and see whether the directory does not already exist. If it does not, we try to create one (line 14), but terminate the program with an appropriate error message if it cannot be created. Please note that the argument to `die` here does not contain a final newline, which means that we would allow the interpreter to append its own error message to ours because we would definitely want to be able to see any system messages that might tell us why we were unable to create the backup folder. If the folder can be created successfully, we report this to the user in line 16. Alternatively, if the folder already exists when we run the program, we also report this (line 20), but take no further action.

The list of files in the source directory is compiled in lines 23–25. However, if, for some reason, we cannot read from our source directory, we again terminate the program with an appropriate message defined by ourselves, plus the corresponding system message. One obvious reason for why we might not be able to read from the source directory is that the user may have specified an incorrect, non-existing path. This may, for example, be a path on a Windows system like 'C:\temp', which might appear perfectly correct until we remember that the character sequence \t will always be interpreted as a tab by perl in double quoted strings, so that – effectively – the path name that the interpreter gets to see consists of 'C:' + tab + 'emp' ('C: emp'), rather than the correctly escaped form 'C:\\temp', where perl is forced to interpret the backslash as a literal character. Now you also know why I suggested earlier that you always use a slash as a path separator, even if you are only ever planning to run your programs on a Windows machine.

Finally, in lines 28–29, we iterate over each of the filenames in the `@files` array in turn. Remember that it is just the bare filenames stored in the array, though, which is why, for both input and output files that we open in lines 32 and 33, respectively – and close again in line 37 – we need to prepend the source and target paths first. In case one of these files cannot be opened for some reason, we simply emit a warning this time, so that the user can be made aware of the fact that something went wrong, but we do not necessarily want to terminate the whole backup operation just because one or two files can potentially not be copied. The actual copy process consists of reading in each file line by line and writing each line out to the corresponding file with the same name in the backup folder (lines 34–36). However, this copy operation is constrained by the condition in line 30, which ensures that the file we are trying to copy is not a directory, for which we use the negated file test -d. And last, but not least, we also let the user know that the backup is finished (line 40).

As I said above, there are still quite a few improvements that we would need to make to turn the above program into a really fool-proof and comprehensive backup program, but I will leave it up to you to consider where things may still be missing or could go wrong and how you could deal with these issues. As an additional exercise, though, I would suggest that you go back to your earlier programs that required user interaction to see whether they could not be improved by adding some error handling.

There are also three more functions that I would like to talk about in passing here, which are related to the topic of directory handling. The first one is the counterpart to mkdir, rmdir, which allows us to remove a (non-empty) directory. The second one is unlink, which takes a list of files as arguments and removes them, provided that you have the permissions to do so. The third is rename, which allows you to change the name of a file. The latter takes two arguments, the original filename and one to rename the file to. In case the second argument is a filename that belongs to an already existing file, the contents of this file will be overwritten without warning. *As using any of these three functions may lead to data loss if applied without proper prior consideration, I would seriously advise you to use them with caution!*

## 6

IDENTIFYING TEXTUAL PATTERNS (BASIC AND EXTENDED REGULAR EXPRESSIONS)

As we have seen in a previous section when we wrote our little simplified verbform analyser (p. 50), many processing tasks in linguistics involve working with or identifying specific textual patterns, such as *prefixes*, *suffixes* and so on. However, linguistic patterns are obviously not only confined to the level of morphology, but may also apply to the levels of phonology, morpho-syntax, syntax, or any potential combination of these. On the level of syntax, for example, patterns can help us to identify *noun phrases*, multi-word units/constructions (for example, *as far as*), idioms, or even whole sentential categories.

The best way – even better than using substr ☺ – to find linguistic (and other) patterns in most sophisticated programming languages is by using *regular expressions* (or *regexes*, for short). These provide convenient ways of specifying patterns to search for in compact and very flexible ways, ways which are usually much more convenient than the 'suffix-stripping' approach we used for the verbform analyser. In order to understand regexes and their usefulness properly, though, we first need to investigate some of the basic concepts underlying them, each time illustrating these concepts by using appropriate linguistic examples.

6.1 MATCHING

The act of finding/identifying particular combinations of characters or strings in text is usually referred to as *(pattern) matching*. When you use pattern matching in Perl, you essentially check to see whether a specific pattern matches either a complete string or part of it. If a match is found, true is returned, otherwise false, just as with any of the conditions we looked at earlier. The syntax for matching is similar to that of doing an assignment, with two exceptions:

1. the equals sign is followed by a tilde symbol, that is =~.
2. the pattern to match is enclosed in a pair of identical delimiters, usually forward slashes (//), although this can be changed if you prefix the first delimiter by *m*.

Thus, if we wanted to see whether the word *how* was contained in the string variable $string, which contained the string "This is how you can show whether one string is contained in another.", you would specify it in this way: $string =~ /how/; . This would return true because the word we are actually looking for is contained in it. However, it would also return true if we changed the value of $string to "This is the way in which you can show whether one string is contained in another.". In case you are now wondering why this is the case, you need to bear in mind that the matching operation is actually (blindly) looking for the specific combination/sequence of characters that makes up the word *how*, no matter whether they in fact occur as this particular word or as part of a longer sequence, in our case the word *show*, and returns true as soon as it is found an appropriate match (actually, the first one). We shall see later how we can avoid such 'errors'.

Graphically represented, the matching inside these two strings would look as follows, if we use boxes to indicate the matched parts:

1. This is $\boxed{\text{how}}$ you can show whether one string is contained in another.
2. This is the way in which you can s$\boxed{\text{how}}$ whether one string is contained in another.

The basic syntax for regex pattern matching is simple enough, so for now, apart from possibly testing the above in a little program, all we need to do is to take a look at how we can do the opposite, that is, to test whether a given string is **not** contained in another. This is very easy to achieve because all that is required in order to *negate* the matching operation is to change the equals symbol to an exclamation mark, in other words, to change the operator from =~ to !~. However, there are still many more things we need to find out about before we can really make proper use of regexes for linguistic purposes.

6.2 CHARACTER CLASSES

Let us assume you wanted to identify all lines in a text that contain certain forms of irregular verbs, such as *sing* and *ring*. Obviously, in order to do so, you could try a matching operation on each one of the individual forms, but this would be rather inefficient. A much more convenient way is to specify all of the potential variant letters at the same time, which is something that can be done by creating so-called *character classes*. The following sample code illustrates how we can specify the *infinitive, past tense* and *past participle* forms for both of the above words in one compact expression for matching against a variable $string: $string =~ /[rs][aiu]ng/;. As you can see, there are two character classes in our example, both created by specifying the alternatives inside square brackets ([...]), the first one comprising the consonant letters *r* and *s*, and the second one the vowel letters *a*, *i* and *u*. It is important to bear in mind, though, that whatever is contained inside a character class only represent alternatives for one single (character) element at a time and not a sequence of characters. We will later find out about ways of *quantifying* character classes to make them represent more (or even less) than one character at a time, wherever this may be appropriate.

It is again also possible to *negate* this kind of construct, that is, to match against *anything but* what is contained in a class. This is done by adding a *caret* symbol (^)

after the opening square bracket. Thus, the code `$string =~ /str[^u]ng/;` would, for example, match the strings *hamstring, string, stringify, Durmstrang, strangle, stranger, headstrong, strong, stronghold* or *strength*, but not *strung*.

However, character classes need not always be composed of individual characters listed in a row, but may also comprise specific *ranges* or predefined classes, such as \w, which is a shorthand expression for *all word characters*. Ranges are indicated by a hyphen (-), such as in [a-z], which represents the group of all (Latin) lowercase letters. If, alternatively, you ever want to include a literal hyphen in your character class, you need to make sure that you either escape it or – better yet – add it either at the beginning or end of the class definition where it will be unambiguous.

Shorthand expressions, such as \w, are often negated simply by using an uppercase letter instead of the corresponding lowercase one, so that \W is defined as comprising the group of *all non-word characters*.

You can also specify more than one range inside a character class, so, for example, the class [A-Z0-9] could be used to match English postcodes (once you know how to quantify), which are comprised of these letters, numbers and a space (included at the end of the class, but not easily visible here) between them. The range 0-9 in our previous example could also be represented by the predefined class \d, where the *d* stands for *digit* and the space could have been represented by \s, which in fact may comprise not only single (white)spaces, but also *tabs* and various types of line breaks. Perhaps the most versatile class of all is represented by the dot (.), which represents *any character* at all – at least in a standard match.

You may have already noticed by now that many simple characters that occur in natural language may have multiple 'meanings' in programming. Thus, for the *dot*, apart from the normal significance as a *full stop* inside an ordinary string, we have already also seen it in its function as a concatenation operator and now with its third function, representing any character in regexes. The thing to bear in mind with these special characters (also referred to as *metacharacters*) is that, whenever they are used in a literal way in special constructs, you have to make sure that they are actually **escaped** by a preceding backslash because otherwise you could only match a full stop accidentally!

[**Exercise 17**] Now, in order to practise what we have learnt about regexes so far, let us rewrite our earlier 'dir_reading.pl' sample program so that, in addition to the directory name, it will also accept a file extension as a string to allow us to filter out only those files with a given extension. We will call this program 'dir_reading_filtered01.pl' because we will later write a more efficient version of it that will be called 'dir_reading_filtered02.pl'. Before we can write this program in a maximally efficient way, though, we still need to talk about one more thing, which is that it is in fact possible to interpolate a string into a regex match. This is what is going to allow us to use the extension that we retrieve as the second command line argument inside a matching operation immediately.

1. Copy 'dir_reading.pl' to 'dir_reading_filtered01.pl'.
2. Adjust it, so that it will accept two parameters off the command line, the source directory and the extension.

3. Inside the `foreach` loop, use a (post-)modifiying `if`-condition to check whether the current filename matches the extension. If you cannot remember how to do the post-modification, check our earlier 'while_loop_short.pl' program (p. 45), where we used this feature in conjunction with the `last` operator.
4. Inside the match, interpolate the extension into the matching operation, but try to anticipate any potential problems and think about whether you may be able to come up with any solutions to them.
5. Test the program on different folders and with different extensions.

As the instructions above have already hinted at, there may still be a number of problems with this program, depending on how you choose to handle the extension. If you choose to accept a bare extension from the user (let us assume *pl* for listing your Perl programs for the moment), you may actually end up listing unwanted files, such as 'plotting.doc' or 'stoplist.txt', simply because these contain the 'extension', albeit in places where we do not want it to appear. This is of course similar to our earlier problem of the *grapheme sequence* <how> being part of the word *show*. You could now opt for making the user specify the dot that precedes the extension together with it. However, you would then also have to inform them somehow that this dot would need to be escaped because otherwise it would mean 'any character' inside the regex and you would still at least accidentally filter out the second of our two example filenames because the extension is here preceded by an <o>, which is certainly one of the potential arbitrary characters (including the full stop) the regex dot acts as a placeholder for. It would therefore be much safer not to let the user provide the dot and provide it as part of the matching structure – obviously in escaped form – you define inside the program. This will at least *anchor* the match to some extent, but even then there may still be a potential problem because it is technically possible (at least for modern-day operating systems) for any given filename to contain multiple spaces. Thus, for now, we will not actually be able to create a 'perfect' version of our program, at least not until we have learnt more about the concept of anchoring.

You may have noted that there is a certain degree of redundancy in our program, too, because we first read in all the filenames in the given directory and then filter out the ones we want later. Would it not be so much nicer, though, if we could only retrieve those filenames from the system that we really wanted in the first place? Well, in order to be able to do this in our revised version of 'dir_reading_filtered01. pl', 'dir_reading_filtered02.pl', we first need to learn about one more Perl function that will allow us to do the filtering 'on-the-fly'. This function is called `grep` and just like the `map` function we learnt about earlier, it also takes a block or expression as its first argument and a list as its second. Now, as the result returned by the `readdir` command is in fact a list of filenames, we can pipe (redirect) this straight through the `grep` function, with an appropriate filtering pattern as the first argument, and immediately get a filtered file list. You may have spotted earlier, though, that the list of filenames we get back from the system is not necessarily in alphabetical order, so we can do even better and pipe the result of the `grep` operation through the `sort` function, which – by default – returns an 'alphabetically' (or *ASCIIbetically*, to be more precise) sorted list. We will learn more about this function very soon, but I just wanted to introduce it briefly here. Now, if we want a plain listing of all the files, to crown all this, we can pass the result of this last operation through map again and have a fully qualified filename stored in the array without ever needing any intermediate auxiliary arrays. The result of all these operations is shown in the following listing for 'dir_reading_filtered02.pl'.

```
1  ($input_dir,$extension) = (shift,shift);
2  @files = ();
3  opendir $DIR, $input_dir or die "unable to open
   directory $input_dir!\n";
4  @files = map {$input_dir.'/'.$_} sort grep
   /\.$extension/, readdir $DIR;
5  closedir $DIR;
6  print join "\n", @files;
```

The above code may look a little daunting to you and you are certainly not obliged to use such compact code in your programs if you (still) feel uncomfortable about it. However, you should be aware of the fact that this is the kind of idiomatic Perl you may well encounter in code written by more advanced programmers, and you should certainly at least make an effort to understand it, too.

The grep function I introduced above is named after the well-known Unix program 'grep', which allows you to pick lines matching a specific regex pattern from a number of different files, but of course the Perl function should not be confused with this, as it matches and returns items that fit patterns from a list of strings. You may have noticed, too, that – unlike the matching operations on scalars we discussed above – the grep function does not make use of the matching operator =~ but, like some other Perl functions that allow you to use regex patterns, just requires you to specify the pattern inside the forward slashes as delimiters. As a matter of fact, we have already seen (and used), at least one other function that accepts a pattern, which is the split function.

6.3 QUANTIFICATION

Although, in some cases, specifying a character class may be enough to cover a diversity of different patterns (such as for our irregular verbs above), often we really need to be able to specify that items from a given character class may indeed be recurring. Let us take a simple example from phonology, this time. It is well known that the grapheme combination <oo> is most often pronounced as /u:/, but other options – in Received Pronunciation (RP) – may also be /ʊ/ (*foot*), /ʊə/ (old-fashioned *poor*), /ɔ:/ (modern *poor*), /ʌ/ (*flood*) or even /əʊ/ (*brooch*). In order to investigate this, we might want to be able to find all words that contain a double <o> in a text *corpus*, a collection of electronic texts compiled according to specific criteria (see Kennedy 1988: 3–5; or Baker et al. 2006: 48). To achieve our objective, what we could do is open one or more corpus files, take each line in turn, split it into individual words, look at each word to see if it contains a double <o> and, if it does, add it to a hash of words, which we could then `sort` (once we have learnt how to a little later in Chapter 8) and output to a file for investigation. To match the double <o>, we could obviously write a pattern that contained two <o>s, but a far better way is to use a *quantifier* after the pattern, stating that we want to find the same letter twice. Below is a list of these quantifiers, as they can be used in Perl:

- a * following a character (class)/group means it may occur from 0 to an unlimited number of times
- a ? following a character (class)/group means it may be optional or can occur at most once
- a + following a character (class)/group means it has to occur at least once but up to an unlimited number of times
- a curly bracket { . . . } following a character (class)/group specifies a more exact quantification
  - {5} matches exactly five times
  - {5, } matches at least 5 times or up to an unlimited number of times
  - {5,10} matches between 5 and 10 times

Looking at this list, we can see that the quantification method we want to use for our example is to write something like: `if ($word =~ /o{2}/) {...}`. Other examples of things to match using the different quantifiers listed above, each time only giving the pattern and explanation, are:

- `/ice[\-\s]*cream/` matches all three different forms of the compound *ice cream* as they occur in the British National Corpus (BNC), *ice cream*, *ice-cream* and *icecream*.
- `/colou?r/` matches both the British and American variants of the word *colour*.
- `/\s\w+\s/` matches any word or single letter (between whitespace characters).
- `/\s\w{5}\s/` matches any word (between whitespace characters) that is exactly five letters long.
- `/\s\w{5,}\s/` matches any word (between whitespace characters) that is at least five letters long – but potentially also 'endless'.
- /\s\w{5,10}\s/ matches any word (between whitespace characters) that is between five and ten letters long.

Please note that the patterns delimited by whitespace above will only match words that do indeed occur between other words and therefore have spaces around them. These patterns would not match any words that either occur at the beginning or end of a line, or that have any punctuation marks following them!

[**Exercise 18**] In order to test the above quantifiers, let us write a little regex testing program, which we will call 'regex_tester.pl'.

1. Use the `shift` operator to retrieve two arguments from the command line and store them in two variables $string and $pattern for the string to be tested and the pattern to test it against.

2. Use the qr operator to turn the pattern into a precompiled regular expression and assign it to another variable called $match. Hint: The qr (*quote regular*) operator is used like a function, with its argument in matching delimiters; in our case, we will use slashes to show the similarity with the matching operation.

3. Test to see if $string matches $match by interpolating the latter into a matching operation and print out an appropriate message, based on whether the test returns a confirmation or failure. Also interpolate the values for both variables into your message for verification purposes.

When you print out the pattern in your message, you will find that it will (probably) be enclosed in round brackets and prefixed by ?-xism:. Do not worry about this for the moment; we will find out about what this relates to a little further down when we discuss *modifiers*. It may also seem odd to you that we have to use an intermediate variable in which to store the compiled regex and cannot simply use qr and shift together in the very first assignment to $pattern. However, this will not work because qr will otherwise interpret 'shift' not as a command but as a literal string here. Nevertheless, we could still have saved ourselves an extra variable if we wanted to, as we could simply have reassigned the result of qr /$pattern/ back to $pattern.

6.4 GROUPING, ALTERNATION AND ANCHORING

As we have just seen, quantifiers are very useful for specifying relatively compact and concise patterns but, used only with character classes, they may actually be of rather limited value because we are only quantifying 'objects' of one particular type. Sometimes we may want to be able to specify more exact or fixed sequences of characters or classes, though, or even variations of these. If we want to do this, we need to at least have the possibility for *grouping* these sequences together, as well as specifying *alternatives*.

Grouping (beyond character classes) in regular expressions is achieved by surrounding sequences of characters or classes by *round brackets*, which tells Perl to treat them as a fixed unit that may then be used and quantified just like a character class. For listing alternatives, you separate the different options via the *pipe symbol* (|). For example, if we wanted to be able to identify all words that start with one of the negative prefixes {in-}, {im-}, {un-}, {de-} or {dis-}, we could try to specify the following grouped alternatives (although this would obviously also give a fair few false hits): (in|im|un|de|dis)\w+ or, more compactly, (i[nm]|un|d(e|is))\w+. But even if we accept that this would also find words like *interest* or *under* (that do not really start with a negative prefix), this pattern still may not yield the right results in many other cases because it could also match somewhere that is not at the beginning of the string we are trying to match against, as in words like *th|un|de|r* (two potential matches if we were to match repeatedly!) or *turpent|in|e*. In order to be able to specify exactly where we want our pattern to match, we also need to know something about *anchoring*, which is what we will discuss next.

Anchoring simply means that we can specify an environment in which the regex is allowed to match, often a specific position. If you have ever looked at any *phonological rules*, this concept should be familiar to you and you will not be surprised to hear that you can also use regexes to model these rules. The most commonly known forms of anchoring in regular expressions are the caret (^) and the dollar ($) symbols. These allow us to anchor our patterns at the *beginning* of the string to be matched against or at its *end*, respectively. However, this is obviously only going to work either if we only have strings that contain single words or if we have previously extracted these individual words from a larger context, such as a sentence or line. In all other cases, we need to employ a different means of specifying beginnings or ends of words, a means which is a little similar to the whitespace markers (\s) we used previously, which is the (word) *boundary marker* \b.

[**Exercise 19**] Armed with all this knowledge, we can now write a slightly more complex program which will help us to identify whether a given string can actually phonotactically be part of an imaginary (but certainly not impossible) language. This language is one which always uses a relatively fixed syllable structure, where each syllable always starts with a consonant letter, followed by a single vowel letter, plus an optional final consonant letter. We will call this program 'syllables.pl'.

1. Retrieve a word to be tested from the command line and store it in $word. To simplify the program a little so as to not have to deal with upper- and lowercase letters separately, use the lc function to change all input characters to lowercase. Hint: this is possibly by using the lc function together with the shift operator before even assigning to $word.
2. Using the qr operator as before, create two character classes, one containing all the vowel letters and one all the consonant letters, and assign them to $v and $c, respectively.
3. Use the qr operator again, and create a new compiled regular expression consisting of the combinatorial options explained above and assign this new pattern to $syll(able). To do this, use the predefined variables we created immediately above and interpolate them into the pattern.
4. Set up a test to find out if the word provided on the command line fits the syllable structure of our language and print out an appropriate message. Do not forget to specify that our word may be composed of *one or more* syllables, using the appropriate boundary markers.

Please note that I have explicitly referred to vowel and consonant "letters" above and not "phonemes". You may want to think about why for a minute and also look at the sample solution to think about whether it could ever work for a language like English on the phonological – rather than purely graphemic/orthographic – level, too. As an optional exercise, you can modify this program to accept a list of words contained in a file and to process each one in turn, writing out words that fit the structure to one file and those that do not to another.

6.5 MEMORISING

A 'side effect' of using the round brackets for grouping is that whatever is contained inside brackets will in fact be *memorised* by Perl and stored in special numbered variables, starting from $1 for the first matched bracket, $2 for the second and so on. Apart from allowing you to find (erroneously) repeated words in a text in a grammar checker inside a word-processor-like application (where you would actually need to specify the repetitions as \1, \2 and so on), this is highly useful if you want to memorise individual parts of a longer pattern, possibly also to use them as *backreferences* in a substitution later on. The distinction between the backslash and the $ backreference notation is that the former is used to refer to bracketed items *inside* the matching operation itself, whereas the $ variant is used to refer to them in contexts *outside* the match. We will discuss substitutions and their uses in more detail in the next chapter.

6.6 MODIFIERS

Regex patterns can also be modified in various ways to control their behaviour even more. Table 6.1 that lists all the different options that can be used inside matching operations:

Table 6.1   Regex match modifiers

Modifier	Meaning
g	Match globally, that is, find multiple occurrences of the same pattern in a single string
i	Do case-insensitive pattern matching
m	Treat string as 'multiple' lines; ^ and $ can match multiple line starts and ends
s	Treat string as 'single' line; dot (.) now matches newlines, too
o	Compile pattern only once
x	Use extended regular expressions

These options are always specified after the final delimiter. If you remember the odd output from 'regex_tester.pl' above with the ?-xism: prefixed, it should now be clear that this indicates that all these modifiers were switched off in our regex, which is what the minus indicates. The final modifier in the table, x, is one that we want to discuss more extensively next because it provides us with a number of useful features that are not found in basic regexes.

6.7 EXTENDED REGULAR EXPRESSIONS

Extended regexes, as they are implemented in Perl, sometimes make our lives a little easier, and sometimes a bit more complicated, for example if we forget about some tiny details, such as spaces. Here, we will only discuss the features that are most useful for our purposes.

Let us start with the feature already hinted at above, which may cause problems if you forget about it. Extended regexes in Perl actually allow you to embed any number of spaces, line breaks, or even comments in them in order to make the expressions more readable. This may be highly advantageous if you have a fairly complex and long expression, but the downside to it is that you need to make all whitespaces that form part of your expression explicit by using \s or even \s+, because otherwise it will simply – and silently – be ignored. Thus, the regex pattern /in to/x will match the preposition *into*, but not the preposition + infinitive marker in the string *in to* separated by a whitespace. To do this correctly, you would either have to specify the pattern as /in\sto/x instead – or not use the x modifier in the first place.

Another highly useful feature, which allows us to save memory or concentrate only on essential sequences in our match, is the ability to switch off the memorisation that usually comes along with grouping because of the use of round brackets. This is done by adding ?: right after the opening bracket. Thus our prefix pattern from above, without memorisation and including an appropriate boundary anchor, would look like this: \b(?:i[nm]|un|d(?:e|is))\w+.

In fact, the question mark following the opening bracket is the 'trademark' or 'common denominator' of all these extended regex features, including the final four types we want to mention here, positive and negative *lookahead* and positive and negative *lookbehind*. These function like anchors in that they specify that a certain pattern has either to (not) follow or (not) precede a given pattern, but without including it in the match itself.

Table 6.2   Extended regex extensions

Extension	Function	Example
?=	positive lookahead	\ba(?=n\b)
?!	negative lookahead	gold(?!en)
?<=	positive lookbehind	(?<=double\s)hamburger
?<!	negative lookbehind	(?<!ice\s)cream

[**Exercise 20**] In order to test and consolidate our knowledge of regular expressions and how they can be usefully employed, let us now try to write a little toy *concordance* program that will allow us to find textual patterns (expressed as regular expressions) in (single) text files. The program is a very basic concordance utility, without any of the additional features that real concordance programs, such as Wordsmith or AntConc, offer. All our program – called 'concordance01.pl' – will allow us to do is to go through a file, identify lines of this file that match a given pattern and output these lines with an indication of the line number in the source file and the pattern that was matched. Please note that the concept of a concordance we employ here is quite different from what Hammond (2003: 114–18) sees as a concordance, which is simply a listing of the individual words in a given file or corpus. We will deal with creating *word lists* of this type in later sections. Before you can write the program, though, we first need to introduce another one of Perl's special variables, $., which holds the current line number of a given input file. And obviously, you will also need an appropriately long file to test the program with. If you do not already have a suitable file, you can download a number of UTF-8-encoded sample files from the accompanying website of this book at <http://www.euppublishing.com/page/essential_prog_linguistics>. You will also be able to use these with some of the later exercises. Inside the program:

1. Read in three arguments from the command line and store them in the variables $pattern, $input_file, and $output_file.
2. Open two suitable filehandles for $input_file and $output_file, also using appropriate error handling mechanisms.
3. Loop over all the lines in the input file, assigning each one to $line in turn.
4. Set up a test condition to see whether the line matches the pattern, storing the actual match inside a backreference. Hint: brackets!
5. If there is a match, write the line number, a comma + space, the match, a colon + space, and finally the line itself to the output file.
6. Make sure you close all filehandles appropriately.
7. Test your program with a number of different textual patterns you know will occur inside the input file(s).

Although this program already represents a fairly useful utility, it is still less than perfect in the sense that we always extract a whole line, which may be much more context for our *search term* than we really require, apart from the fact that we are not identifying any potential multiple instances of the pattern that may occur on the line and we are also not highlighting the match in a way that would make it easier to see in the output. We will investigate some ways of dealing with these drawbacks in the next section, though, once we know how to modify our results to fit our needs.

[**Exercise 21**] As an additional exercise, create a modified copy of our earlier program 'verbform_tester.pl', called 'verbform_tester_re.pl', so that the conditions no longer make use of the substr function to identify the final character(s), but instead match the appropriately anchored suffix patterns.

7

MODIFYING TEXTUAL PATTERNS
(SUBSTITUTION AND TRANSLITERATION)

In the previous chapter, we saw how to recognise and use regexes in order to test whether a given pattern exists somewhere within a string. However, merely verifying the existence of a particular pattern may not be all we want or need to do. Often, we might really want to modify a given string or text in order to correct errors, to change/convert some existing material into a particular format, or to enrich a text with illustrative information, such as marking up learner errors automatically or adding morphosyntactic information to words or phrases. To modify a text/string in such a way in Perl, we can use *substitution*.

7.1 SUBSTITUTION

Substitution combines the identification (matching) of patterns in strings with instructions for making changes to them accordingly. For example, if we wanted to change all definite articles in a text to indefinite ones in order to see how this affects the *coherence* of this text, we could read in the source text and write it out again, just as we did with our little copy program earlier, but instead of simply outputting each line we would change all occurrences of *the* to *a* before printing, using the following syntax (assuming that we are using $line instead of $_): $line =~ s/\bthe\b/a/g;. Obviously, we would also have to add a few more substitutions to cater for sentence-initial capital *The*, as well as to take care of cases where the next word might start with a vowel letter. Although this is a relatively simple substitution example, we can make it even more obvious what the search term and the replacement are by adding some comments and spacing to it, provided we use the x modifier:

```
$line =~ s/
  # string to be replaced, including appropriate
boundary markers
  # also use negative lookahead to exclude cases where
the next word
  # starts with a vowel letter
  \bthe(?!\s[aeiou])\b
  /a/xg; # replacement string, note global replacement
modifier, too!
```

As you can see, essentially a substitution looks like a matching operation – because that is what the first part is – the only differences being that you need to add an s before the first pattern delimiter and a replacement string for whatever has been matched, terminated by a third delimiter of the same type. Note that in our example we have also added the g modifier because otherwise only every first occurrence of our pattern would be replaced on each line. As with the normal matching operation, it is also possible to change the delimiters. However, if you want to do this using different start and end markers, you may need to use four delimiters instead of three, as in $line =~ s{\bthe\b(?!\s[aeiou])}{a}xg;. Using the form of commenting we saw above is especially useful if we are using fairly complex constructs, but you always need to bear in mind that the comments and freeform spacing can only occur in the matching part because most of the substitution content – apart from any potential backreferences (or programming constructs we are not going to discuss) – is generally interpreted as a literal string.

Now that we know how to do substitution, we can also solve the problem of different line endings on different operating systems that we discussed in section 4.1. The solution that Wall et al. (2000: 623) suggest is the following format, that we can apply to our variable $line like this $line =~ s/\015?\012/\n/, to translate all operating system-specific line endings into "logical newlines" (ibid.: 622). Note the octal representation of the characters here, as their logical equivalents \r and \l, could be misinterpreted by the operating system.

Because matching and substitution are such important operations in linguistic analysis and processing, let us do three more exercises now. [**Exercise 22**] As the first one, write a short program, called 'coherence_exercise.pl', which, instead of replacing one type of article by another, removes all articles in the whole text, leaving appropriate gaps. Make sure that the matching part finds all articles at the same time by specifying a suitable alternation pattern. In addition, write the program so that it will require only one command line argument, the input filename, and automatically generates an output filename, such as *filename*_gap.*txt*, from this using the substr function.

As the second and third exercises, we will modify and enhance our earlier concordance program. [**Exercise 23**] In the first of these modified versions, called 'concordance02.pl', we will add only a single improvement, which is to highlight the search term in the output line by substituting it by whatever was matched – using a backreference – and >>> and <<< for the highlighting. By highlighting the match inside the string that holds the line's content, we can also save ourselves printing out the match after the line number. Just like the previous exercise, this one should by now be simple enough for you to write without any additional explanations, but we will discuss the second improved version in more detail.

As I said earlier, a line-based approach to concordancing may not be the best option, as frequently it may give us too much context. Sometimes, though, it may also not provide us with enough context, for instance, if the text file we are running the concordance on has redundant line breaks in it, simply because of formatting decisions its creators have made or because they wanted to be faithful to an original book format. This is why most concordancing tools opt for a *stream-based* approach instead of a line-based one. We already nearly know how to achieve this because what we will need to do in the first instance is to slurp the file into a string. This, however, will still not allow us to treat the text in the way we want to use it because there will still be unwanted newlines in it, which we need to remove. However, if we simply replace all newlines by nothing, we may also involuntarily create new 'compounds' because not all lines will end in a space and some line-final and line-initial words may therefore be 'concatenated' by a removal operation. The safest approach therefore is to replace all newlines by a space and then, in the next step, all multiple spaces by single ones, as shown in the following piece of code.

```
1  for ($file_content) {
2        # remove all newlines and replace them by
         spaces, just in case there are line breaks
         without spaces between words
3        s/\n/ /xg;
4        # collapse all multiple spaces potentially
         caused by the above into a single one
5        s/\s+/ /xg;
6  }
```

There is one more thing that requires explaining in the above code, which is the syntax of the unusual for loop. In all previous for loops, we always used to iterate over a list of elements, while here we only find a single scalar variable, which incidentally contains the text of the file that was slurped in. If you look closely at the substitutions within the loop, you will also notice that there does not seem to be any string argument for the substitution operations. This, however, is not true because what this special one-element for loop actually does is to contextualise $file_contents, so that all following operations are implicitly performed on it. This approach can save us a lot of typing, apart from being less error prone, especially if there are multiple substitutions as would, for example, be the case in a file conversion program.

Our next task is to find all occurrences of our search pattern in $file_contents, which we can do using a while loop in which we repeatedly try to match the pattern, storing a backreference to it. Each time we find a match inside the loop, we can then store its contents inside a temporary variable, which we shall call $match. The contents of the match will always be accessible via the backreference $1. Each time a match is found, its end position (offset) inside the string we are matching against will be stored and can be retrieved via the pos function. Because our pattern may in fact match strings of variable length if we use any quantification, we need to store the starting points of the matches, as well as the length of the matched string, so that we can later extract them from the text (string), together with however much context we choose to specify. In order to store these two items of information, we use two synchronised arrays, each time pushing the length of the match onto an array called @ends and the starting position – computed from whatever the pos function returns, minus the length of the match – onto the end of the @starts array. The following piece of code will help us to achieve the things described above:

```
1  while ($file_content =~ /($pattern)/gx) {
2         # save the match because it may be of variable
          length and we need to know starting point and
          length to retrieve context
3         $match = $1;
4         # store the length in the end array
5         push @ends, length ($match);
6         # store the beginning of the match, so we can
          compute left context later
7         push @starts, (pos($file_content)
          - length($match));
8  }
```

The temporary variable $match is not absolutely needed here because we could just as well compute the length of the match from $1. However, I personally prefer to use it as a safeguarding mechanism because $1 easily gets overwritten by any other matching operations that may be added somewhere to the code at a later point in time.

In the next step, we can then extract the matches, based on their starting and end positions recorded in the arrays. However, as we want to be able to view not only the matches but also some appropriate context that the user can specify, we need to calculate new start and end positions that include this context. For our display, we also want to have the match printed in the centre, so we choose to make the context equal on both sides, as well as adding the highlighting again, once we have extracted the results. There is, however, still one further problem here, which is that there may not actually be enough context available if the match occurs near the beginning or end of the text. In this way, to still be able to display the match in the centre, we need to calculate and add some appropriate *padding* in the form of whitespace to the left. The relevant code to achieve this – including some comments and commented-out debug statements – is shown below again:

```
1  # establish how many elements we have in the array
   of hits
2  my $hits = scalar @starts;
3  # iterate over all hits
4  for ($hit = 0;$hit <= $hits-1;$hit++) {
5         $padding = 0;
6         # extract relevant substring from file
          contents string
7         # starting offset = match position, length =
          length of match + 2 * context
8         # if match position - context is negative...
```

```
9        $start = $starts[$hit]-$context;
10       if ($start =~ /^-/x) {
11           #print "negative start: $start\n";
12           $padding = 0-$start;
13           #print $padding,"\n";
14           $start = 0;
15       }
16       $result = substr($file_
         content,$start,$ends[$hit]+ 2 * $context);
17       # add 'match highlight'
18       $result =~ s/($pattern)/>>> $1 <<</gx;
19       #print "start position= ",$starts[$hit]-
         $context, " end position=
         ",$ends[$hit]+$context,"\n\n";
20       print $OUT " " x $padding, $result,"\n\n";
21   }
```

This code should not require much further comment, although it may well take you a while to understand it completely. There are nevertheless a few more features that may merit additional explanations. The if condition in line 10 checks to see whether the result of the calculation in line 9, stored in $start, has a negative prefix. This can be established using the regex above because a negative number in fact starts with a minus prefix/sign. Subtracting a negative integer from 0 will turn the result into a positively signed integer, which will then be the number of characters required for padding. If the starting position is negative, we also set it to 0 in line 14, after having calculated the padding because that is where we want to start extracting text from in the substr operation in line 16. And finally, in the print operation in line 20, we use another new construct, the x operator, which repeats the preceding string argument – in our case a space – as many times as specified by numerical argument that follows the x. [**Exercise 24**] To complete this exercise now, copy the code parts presented above into 'concordance03.pl' and complete the program using your own knowledge of file slurping and substitution.

7.2 GREEDINESS

Substitution is also a very useful means of changing or removing the formatting/ layout of a given text or part of it. Often, it is used in order to clean up text that is marked up in some specific way, such as web pages, which are usually written in HTML (**Hypertext Markup Language**). If this is done improperly, however, it may even lead to loss of information due to a feature of many 'open-ended' quantifiers which is called *greediness*. Especially when specifying patterns using the * and + quantifiers, and mostly in conjunction with the . (any character) character class, we need to pay particular attention to ensure that we do not end up with matches that include far too many characters and therefore delete more than we actually intended to. Luckily, turning a greedy regex into the corresponding non-greedy one is relatively simple, because – apart from constructing a sensible pattern in the first place – all you need to do is add a ? after the quantifier.

[**Exercise 25**] In order to demonstrate the effect of greediness, let us write another program ('substitute_html.pl') that uses a greedy and a non-greedy match for identifying the pattern to be removed from a line of HTML tagged data. Before we do this, however, I shall first provide a very brief, sometimes (perhaps over-)simplified, introduction to markup languages in general for those readers who are unfamiliar with them. More advanced readers may wish to skip straight to doing the exercise.

7.3 A VERY BRIEF INTRODUCTION TO MARKUP LANGUAGES (SGML, HTML AND XML)

In the 1960s, first attempts were made to create standardised ways of exchanging information on the computer. These eventually led to the ratification of the first 'official' markup language, SGML (Standard Generalized Markup Language) by the ISO (International Standards Organization) in 1986 (cf. Bradley 1998: 6). Since then, a number of other markup languages have developed out of SGML, most notably HTML as the 'language of the web', and a modernised and more flexible version of SGML, called XML (eXtensible Markup Language). Both of these keep evolving and exist in different versions, the latest version of HTML, XHTML, in fact being a dialect of XML. What all of these SGML-derivatives have in common is that they contain plain text along with so-called *elements*, often also referred to as *tags*, although these should of course not be confused with the kind of morpho-syntactic *annotation* that we find in part-of-speech-annotated linguistic data. To distinguish these elements from the plain text, their contents are enclosed in angled brackets (< . . . >).

There are essentially two different types of elements, 'paired' ones that enclose some other content (such as plain text or larger textual divisions), or specific processing instructions for programs that can handle them. We will illustrate these using a suitable number of examples to help us understand how HTML works. 'Paired' elements have corresponding *start* and *end* tags; the most common example in HTML is represented by the *paragraph* element, with its start tag <p> and the corresponding end tag </p>. The forward slash that follows the opening angled bracket is one of the things that distinguishes end from start tags. Within the paragraph tag, we can have other paired elements that either mark off smaller textual (logical) units called *spans* (. . .) or mark off parts of the text to apply specific formatting or markup options to them, for example . . . for *bold* or <i>. . .</i> for *italics*, although some HTML purists prefer to use their logical equivalents . . . or . . . instead. This is because the logical variants make less explicit prescriptions as to the exact formatting and browsers can (theoretically) interpret and render them in different ways, or their exact formatting can be defined via so-called *style sheets*.

A further important element in HTML is the *anchor* (<a>), which contains a descriptive text between the start and end tags, as well as (minimally) a *hypertext reference* (href) *attribute* that contains the address of a web page that is linked to. Attributes like this can only occur in the start tags of paired elements and can contain various types of information, such as where a linked-in resource is to be found, a particular identifier for the element and so forth. They are always made up of two parts, joined together by an equals sign, where the first part represents the attribute *name* and the second part its *value* (like the key-value pairs in hashes), which has to be enclosed in single or double quotes, similar to strings in Perl. An example of an element with a single attribute would be `<div id="chapter01">` (see below).

At the same level in the textual hierarchy as paragraphs, we also find paired tags for six different levels of headings `<h1>` through `<h6>`, and there is one more text element above these, which is the *division* (`<div>`), which can be used to group headings and paragraphs into larger units like *sections* or *chapters*. An HTML document is also further divided into two parts, a *header* (`<head>`) and a *body* (`<body>`) element. The former contains meta-information, such as the *title*, *encoding*, or other information about the document, while the latter comprises all the textual content elements we discussed before. Head and body in turn are wrapped in an `<html>` container element and may be preceded by a *document type declaration*, but generally browsers will also display HTML documents without these correctly. In the case of an XHTML document, the document type declaration should also be preceded by an *XML declaration*.

Thus, the most basic HTML structure would look as follows, where ... indicates any arbitrary content and the indentation the level within the hierarchy:

```
<html>
  <head>
    <title>...</title>
  </head>
  <body>
    <h1>...</h1>
    <p>...</p>
    <h2>...</h2>
    <p>...</p>
    <p>...</p>
  </body>
</html>
```

Non-paired elements are used for including processing instructions. These can take the form of declarations, such as the ones referred to above, but more often, at least inside the `<body>`, they consist of so-called 'empty' elements; 'empty' because they contain no textual data. The tags for these empty elements in XHTML always need to have a slash before the closing angled bracket, for example `<br />` for inserting a manual line break or `<img src="./example.gif" />` for including a graphic called 'example.gif' inside the document at the place where the element occurs.

The original forms of HTML used to be highly restricted with regard to their possible elements. At the same time, HTML also used to be very 'forgiving' as far as case was concerned; it was quite possible to mix upper- and lowercase freely to refer to the same element and the browser would still display the document correctly. XML, and with it XHTML, is less flexible in this respect, but much more flexible in contrast in that it allows the user to define *new* – preferably self-explanatory – element names – hence eXtensible. Of course, it is then up to the user to also define how this particular element is to be rendered, often via a style sheet.

The only thing that is absolutely necessary for an XML document is that it must be *well formed*. This means that the document needs to start with an XML declaration, followed by a freely definable container element, that all paired elements must have appropriate start and end tags, that no paired elements may overlap and that all attribute values are properly quoted. It is possible, though, to constrain the content of XML documents further via *document type* (DTD) or *schema definitions*, in which case they need to follow these specifications exactly in order to be *valid*.

Armed with this knowledge about markup languages and their form, we can now proceed to do our exercise.

1. Create a variable $html_string1 and initialise it to "This   is   a test string in html for <i>testing</i> greediness in substitutions.".
2. Copy $html_string1 to another variable $html_string2.
3. Print out the original string, together with an informative message, for reference purposes. Add newlines appropriately to separate your message from the string.
4. Modify $html_string1 by substituting **every** possible HTML tag, that is any pair of angled brackets with **one or more** arbitrary characters inside them by nothing.
5. Do the same thing for $html_string2, but this time constraining your match to turn it into a non-greedy one.
6. Print out appropriate descriptive messages for both strings, along with the values of the modified strings, again 'formatting' your output in an appropriate manner to make it easier to identify the results.

What you should be able to see immediately when you run this program is that the greedy substitution 'eats up' far more text than we had intended, thereby completely 'changing' the meaning of the original text and rendering it incoherent, whereas the non-greedy variant does exactly what we wanted it to do:

```
The original string was:
This is a <b>test</b> string in html for <i>testing</
i> greediness in substitutions.
This is the result of the greedy match substitution:
This is a greediness in substitutions.
This is the result of the non-greedy match
substitution:
This is a test string in html for testing greediness
in substitutions.
```

7.4 TRANSLITERATION

Transliteration is 'the little brother' of substitution. Unlike substitution, which can replace fixed or variably specified sequences of characters, it essentially creates a fixed mapping from one character to another, based on a list of characters to *search* for and a corresponding list to *replace* them with – at least in its simple form. It does not allow any interpolation, either, so – unfortunately – you cannot predefine strings that contain the elements to be replaced and those to replace them, or easily adapt them later on. The `tr` operator in Perl provides the simple replacement functionality, plus a few more complex operations. Although transliteration is not an operation that employs regexes, it nevertheless uses the `=~` operator in order to bind the string to be manipulated to the `tr` function. So, for example, if you wanted to test for the existence of possible *minimal pairs* for some English words by exchanging vowel graphemes, you could write something like the following: `$string = "big bog bot bad bid bit did dad dog git got";` `$string =~ tr/iao/uei/;` and check the result for valid forms. If you wanted to replace all forms of <e>, <i> and <a> by <o>, you could simply make the second (replacement) list contain only a single element, which would then be used to replace each item in the search list as in: `$string = "far feed feel feet pit tip turn";` `$string =~ tr/eiau/o/;`, resulting in `"for food fool foot pot top torn"`, retaining any duplicated characters. Texts modified in this way could, again, be used in order to investigate either potential minimal pairs or how typing errors may influence the comprehensibility/coherence of texts.

To practise basic transliteration, let us write a little utility that will allow us to – at least partially – convert a pseudo-phonetic representation called SAMPA (**S**peech **A**ssessment **M**ethods **P**honetic **A**lphabet; cf. <http://www.phon.ucl.ac.uk/SAMPA/SAMPA computer readable phonetic alphabet.htm>) to proper IPA. This method of representation was originally devised because it was difficult to represent phonetic characters on the computer in 7- or 8-bit character sets without using some specialised fonts, but has become somewhat redundant since Unicode has established itself more and more by now. As it is still a little difficult to produce phonetic characters via the keyboard, unless one has a proper utility, we will use a different way of representing our phonetic symbols in the conversion program, which is via their code points. In Perl, you can insert any Unicode character in a program, provided that you know its code point, using the special notation \x{code point}. Table 7.1 overleaf lists the most commonly used symbols for English. Only those letters that do not form part of the original Latin alphabet are listed here, as all the Latin-based ones remain the same, anyway.

[**Exercise 26**] Using the code points from Table 7.1, you should now be in a position to complete our exercise called 'sampa_to_ipa.pl', based on the following instructions.

1. Define a variable called `$sampa_string` and initialise it to `D@lQNbraUn@NgreIlaIn`.

Table 7.1   SAMPA to IPA conversion table

SAMPA	IPA	Code Point
I	ɪ	026A
E	ɛ	025B
3	ɜ	025C
@	ə	0259
A	ɑ	0251
V	ʌ	028C
Q	ɒ	0252
O	ɔ	0254
U	ʊ	028A
:	ː	02D0
T	θ	03B8
D	ð	00F0
S	ʃ	0283
Z	ʒ	0292
r	ɹ	0279
N	ŋ	014B

2. Copy the contents of `$sampa_string` to `$ipa_string`.
3. Use the `tr` operator to replace all the SAMPA characters given in Table 7.1 by their Unicode IPA equivalents.
4. Open an output filehandle for the UTF-8-encoded file 'phon_conversion.txt'.
5. Print two messages to the file, one that shows the original value of the SAMPA string and one that does the same for the new IPA string, both including some descriptive text.
6. Close the filehandle again, run the program, and test the result.

The output should look somewhat like this:

```
SAMPA string before conversion: D@lQNbraUn@NgreIlaIn
IPA string equivalent after conversion:
ðəlɒŋbɹaʊnəŋgɹeɪlaɪn
```

Of course, this program will only allow you to convert a limited amount of SAMPA transliteration, but you can always expand it to fit your needs if you should come across some SAMPA-encoded data that contains other character transliterations, or if you just quickly want to create a phonetic transcription yourself without having to insert the phonetic characters painstakingly from the Windows character map or some other such facility on Linux. All you would have to do to make the program more easily usable is to change it to accept SAMPA input from the command line or to modularise it in some other way to allow you to call it from another program, once we have learnt how to create modular programs. Although such a utility program is fairly handy, it is obviously much nicer to be able to use the proper phonetic characters in your programs, for example, if you are working on some grapheme-to-phoneme converter or similar program or you want to create a pronunciation dictionary. In this case, it is also possible to use UTF-8 characters in your program text directly, provided that you add the statement use utf8; at the top of your program before your own code, but after the shebang line. We will learn more about the significance of use in a later section.

Just as for regex matching and substitution, there are also some modifiers that can be used with the tr operator, namely:

Table 7.2　Transliteration modifiers

Modifier	Function
c	complement pattern
d	delete unreplaced characters
s	squash duplicate characters

We will only look at an example of complementation here, as it illustrates nicely how you can demonstrate the *phonotactic* patterns of consonants, as well as the combinability of vowel letters in English (or any other language that employs a similar alphabet). In order to highlight these patterns, we can simply specify the following bit of code: $string =~ tr/iaou /C/c;, which will turn the string "far feed string texts buses" into "CaC CeeC CCCiCC CeCCC CuCeC", replacing all but the vowel letters and spaces by a placeholder for consonants. Of course, as usual with our short, simplified sample programs, this program is still less than perfect from a phonological point of view, but you can always think about ways of improving it...

## 8

GETTING THINGS INTO THE RIGHT ORDER
(BASIC SORTING)

Sorting data is an important task in many different areas of linguistics programming, especially when dealing with things such as frequency lists or alphabetical word lists, similar to the ones contained in dictionaries. Other operations that may require the sorting of data are statistical evaluations, where it is often necessary to sort and group data in order to determine the most significant items, for example, in order to establish sample *medians* or *modes*. The simplest form that sorting operations can take is simply to put the words in a list into alphabetic order, as the following small program will illustrate:

```
1  @unsorted_words = @ARGV;
2  @sorted_words = sort @unsorted_words;
3  foreach $word (@sorted_words) {
4    print $word, "\n";
5  }
```

You can copy the above program to a file named 'simple_sort.pl' and experiment with it by providing a few words starting with different letters on the command line.

1. Begin by inputting only lowercase words.
2. Next, try a combination of upper- and lowercase letters, where the ones starting with uppercase letters should ideally be ones that come further back in the alphabet.
3. And finally, try test the program with a series of numbers consisting of 1 to 3 digits.

Let us discuss the program and the test results you should have observed. First of all, it should have become quite clear that achieving a basic alphabetic sorting – at least according to the alphabetical order computers use by default– is easily achieved by using the sort function with an array as its (sole) argument and assigning the result to another array. However, when doing exercise 2, you should have noted that the computer sees alphabetic ordering as an ordering according to ASCII code numbers (or Unicode code points). If you remember, this is exactly the same phenomenon we already observed when we introduced the eq operator in the section on flow control. This, though, is quite different from what a human user of the computer would see as a proper alphabetical order, namely, that of dictionary order, where no distinction should be made between upper- and lowercased words, so that they should be sorted together. And last, but not least, exercise 3 should have demonstrated to you that the default alphabetical sorting of numbers will not actually give us the right numerical order, but an order that will only depend on the codes the individual number characters have in the ASCII table, so that, for example, 12 and 23 will always be sorted before 3 because the initial 1 and 2 respectively in the former two numbers occur before the 'initial' 3.

8.1 KEYS AND SORT ORDER

Our earlier simple example was based on the assumptions that

1. we have only one *sort criterion* or *key*;
2. we actually want to sort things in *ascending* order; and
3. we want to sort according to what constitutes an alphabet to the computer.

In practice, though, it is often the case that we may want to employ different sort keys, for example, in sorting word frequency lists first 'alphabetically' and then in *descending* number of occurrence (frequency) and so on. So how do we overcome this apparent problem? Simply by adding another argument to the sort function, usually in the form of a comparison block (although it could also be a subroutine, which we will learn about later), before specifying the name of the array. The reason why we can do this is because, internally, Perl always uses two implicit variables $a and $b for comparison, anyway, and we can control the sorting behaviour by either changing their *order of comparison* or the *operator* used for comparing them.

Although there are different ways to achieve different types of comparison, we will only discuss the most straightforward ones, first making a distinction between the operators used for 'alphabetical' and numerical comparison, and then working out what to do in order to reverse the sorting direction. The operator used for doing 'alphabetical' comparisons is relatively easy to remember because it is just an abbreviated form of the word *compare* or *comparison*, cmp. Its numerical counterpart is essentially a composite form of all the different numerical comparison options, less than (<), greater than (>) and equals (=), that is <=>, sometimes also more colloquially referred to as the 'spaceship operator' because it looks like one of the fighter ships from *Star Wars*.

As already hinted at above, we can use the position of the two auxiliary variables to specify the direction of sorting. In a sense, this makes it easier to write comparisons because we do not always have to think about which way round 'the arrow' needs to point, but simply swap the order of the two variables to change direction.

Thus, in order to do a numerical rather than an alphabetical comparison, we change the line where we do the sorting above to @sorted_words = sort {$a <=> $b} @unsorted_words; and it will sort any numbers that we provide as arguments correctly in ascending order. [**Exercise 27**] You can verify this by copying 'simple_sort.pl' to 'simple_sort_nums.pl' and testing it with a set of numbers again. If you want to reverse the sort order to descending order, then you can change it to @sorted_words = sort {$b <=> $a} @unsorted_words; instead. In case you want to sort words in descending alphabetical order, though, you can use the cmp comparison operator for 'alphabetical' comparison and simply reverse $a and $b, as in @sorted_words = sort {$b cmp $a} @unsorted_words;.

As the two variables $a and $b are in fact aliases for the items to be compared, but not the items themselves, we can also do very neat things with them. For instance, if we are comparing words alphabetically, we can pretend that both words are in lowercase by using the lc function to manipulate $a and $b inside the sorting block. Thus, the syntax @sorted_words = sort {lc($a) cmp lc($b)} @unsorted_words; will allow us to create a *dictionary-sorted* list of words where upper- and lowercase words are sorted together, rather than all uppercase words appearing first and then all lowercase ones later.

Now that we have learnt about basic sorting, we can move on to creating simplified word or vocabulary lists from texts in our next section.

8.2 'VOCABULARY HANDLING' (CREATING SIMPLE WORD LISTS)

Computers are ideally suited to creating vocabulary lists because they can go through many files in a matter of seconds only, extract all words, and create lists out of them. This may then form the basis for dictionary development, comparing existing word lists to new ones in order to identify domain-specific vocabulary, creating a list of vocabulary items to learn or to spot new words that have recently entered a language and so on. Here, we will employ our newly developed knowledge of how to sort arrays, together with our recently developed expertise in substitution, in order to produce such lists in a fairly lengthy exercise. After having completed the exercise, we will also discuss the efficiency of the approach taken in order to create the list.

Before beginning this exercise, though, we need to discuss some of the issues involved in processing text files in order to extract suitable vocabulary items. As we all know, text files not only consist of words but also of all sorts of potential formatting or structuring options (as we have seen in our exercise on greediness and the discussion of markup languages, as well as punctuation marks and other symbols, such as quotation marks, hyphens/dashes, brackets and many more. Before arriving at our list of words therefore, we first need to remove all of these, at the same time making sure that we do not accidentally remove any unwanted items or join words together when taking out specific items. The basic maxim therefore always ought to be: ***If in doubt, always test your substitutions in order to avoid any negative side effects!***

Furthermore, if we simply extract all words from one or more texts, store them in an array and sort them, we will still not end up with a proper vocabulary list because most words – or word *types*, to be more exact – usually do not occur only once in a text, so that we actually need to remove duplicate *tokens* from the initial list in order to arrive at the final 'product'. [**Exercise 28**] Bearing all these issues in mind, we can now begin to write our vocabulary list generator, which we will call 'simple_vocab.pl'.

1. Declare two empty arrays named @words and @vocab_list.
2. Set up a variable to hold the name of an input file and initialise it by retrieving a single command line argument.

3. Add some error handling which prints out an appropriate message in case no command line argument has been provided by the user.
4. Set up a filehandle and try to open the file specified on the command line, again providing appropriate error handling in case the file cannot be opened.
5. Set up a `while` loop to iterate over the filehandle, each time storing the line retrieved by the diamond operator in `$line`.
6. Make sure you remove all end of line markers (newlines).
7. Skip any empty lines.
8. Process each line in turn.
   a. Replace all unwanted characters.
   b. Remove any leading or trailing whitespace that may have been created through the substitution operation.
   c. Use the `split` function to split the current line at one or more whitespaces and assigning the result to an array called `@elements`.
   d. Use the `push` function to append `@elements` to `@words`.
9. Do not forget to close the input filehandle, as it is no longer needed now.
10. Sort `@words` and assign it back to itself.
11. For reference purposes, print out the word list so far, in order to see how many duplicates there are and to verify that it has been successfully sorted.
12. Establish the length of `@words` and store the result in `$array_length`.
13. Set up a `for` loop (using `$i` as a counter variable) to iterate over all elements of `@words`.
14. Inside the loop,
   a. first assign the $(\$)i^{th}$ element of the array to `$a` and the $(\$)i+1^{th}$ element to `$b`;
   b. next, test to see whether the contents of `$a` and `$b` are not equal and, if so, push `$a` onto the `@vocab_list` array.
15. Add a `print` statement to your code that separates the original word list from the final vocabulary list, also providing an appropriate 'heading' for the latter.
16. Print out the vocabulary list and compare it to the end of the original one to verify whether your loop was set up correctly and all elements have been processed.
17. Test the program with one or more sample files from the accompanying website.

The above program will certainly work relatively well on smaller files or even a set of them, if suitably modified in order to accept multiple files as arguments. However, when dealing with larger amounts of text, we will create larger and larger arrays of words that will be highly redundant and require much more processing effort than actually needed. Thus, although this is one possible way of achieving our end, it is certainly not the most efficient and we mainly wrote it to get some more practice in cleaning up files, sorting and working with arrays. We will soon see a way of avoiding this inefficiency, though, when we discuss how to create *word frequency lists*.

The above program will also work well on the command line if you are processing files that only contain the basic Latin characters, but if you want to use it for handling Unicode you should definitely write the output to a suitable filehandle.

9

ELEMENTARY TEXTS STATS
(CREATING BASIC FREQUENCY LISTS)

Doing basic descriptive statistics on text data generally involves at least some of the elements of creating word lists like the one we produced in the preceding section, although the unit of the word will not always be the one that we are interested in investigating. Depending on the *tokenisation* of our textual data, we can also research and describe the behaviour of larger units, such as multi-word units or idioms, paragraphs, sentences and so forth. For some of these, some more *pre-processing* of the data may be necessary than in our latest example. Thus, for example, if we want to investigate multi-word units and their frequencies along with basic single-word tokens, we may first need to identify them inside a text using pattern-matching techniques and *mask* them in some way, for instance, by replacing the spaces between them by underscores, so that later sentence-splitting operations that may be based on spaces between words will not count them as their individual elements. When handling texts on a paragraph-by-paragraph basis, for example, in analysing textual complexity, we can either extract the relevant units by using *paragraph mode* when reading in the file or relying on explicit markup – such as HTML paragraph or heading tags – to identify the relevant units. Of course, we can also research units that are below the level of the word, such as we have seen in our earlier example of where we extracted each nth character to test and see whether it was an *e*. We could, for example, split a text into its individual characters in the same way, then count the occurrences of each character and try to identify the language it was written in because the frequency of letters (or phonemes), along with possibly their sequencing, is often indicative of a particular language.

The exact steps we may need to perform in preparing our data may be quite complex and will often depend on the exact nature of the data, but essentially all the basic steps will always remain the same and will consist of a combination of matching, substitution and splitting operations.

9.1 COMPLEX SORTING

Whenever we deal with more elaborate data than simple lists of words, we also need to employ more complex types of sorting to be able to analyse and somehow make explicit the nature of our data. In simple one-word or one-element lists, there is essentially only one key or sorting criterion, either the alphabetical sequence of characters or the numerical value of an item. At the next level of complexity in our hierarchy is the (simple) hash, where we already minimally need to make a choice between one of two options for specifying our sorting keys, either the *hash key* or its *associated value*. This level of 'complexity' could potentially increase even further if we were to deal with more complex (compound) data types, such as arrays stored inside other arrays or inside hashes, or hashes stored inside arrays and so on. We will deal with these problems as they may arise in our programs, but for now we want to concentrate on and illustrate processing 'straightforward' hashes, used in order to produce *frequency lists*.

9.2 WORD FREQUENCY LISTS

Word frequency lists are essentially very similar to the type of word list that we produced in the previous section, only that each *word form* or token also has an associated frequency value that reflects how often it occurs in a given corpus, and that there are multiple ways of looking at – that is sorting and outputting/displaying – such a list. The four basic options for sorting word frequency lists are:

- sorted according to **keys** (words forms) in **ascending** order ⇒ A-z
- sorted according to **keys** (words forms) in **descending** order ⇒ z-A
- sorted according to **values** (word frequency) in **ascending** order ⇒ 1-n
- sorted according to **values** (word frequency) in **descending** order ⇒ n-1

Each of the above can theoretically also be sorted using a secondary key, based on its complementary part, that is, when sorting according to keys, we can follow this by another sort according to values and vice versa, where each time we also have the option to reverse the sort order again, depending on our needs.

A further, somewhat lesser-used, option for word frequency lists is a *reverse sorted* list, which can be used to investigate *suffix* patterns. In producing such a list, all words that are part of it are first reversed, then sorted and counted, and then reversed again for output, so that for example all *-ing forms* or all *adverbs* ending in *–ly* appear 'next to' each other.

9.3 IMPLEMENTING A LIST

Implementing the frequency list to some extent involves the same procedures we used for creating our (inefficient) word list, although now we use a single hash for storing the words instead of an array. Again, we need to open one filehandle at a time, process all lines and store the words in a temporary array. However, instead of appending each temporary array of words to the existing array of words for later processing, this time we actually iterate over the array immediately, 'check' to see whether the word form exists as a hash key and increase a counter associated with this key. Since hash keys have to be *unique*, a simple `foreach` loop, assuming that we have already set up a hash called `%words` and are still using `@elements` as our temporary array of words, will do this job:

```
1  foreach $word (@elements) {
2      $words{$word}++;
3  }
```

Line 2 of the example may need a little bit of explaining. The ++ bit simply means that a numerical variable is incremented by1. This implicit numerical variable that we are using here is associated with $words{$word}, in other words the value associated with the key represented by the current word form retrieved from the array. Now, because each hash key has to be unique, every time that the Perl interpreter encounters the word form, it increases the existing counter by1. In other words, the syntax we have used corresponds to the longer form of $words{$word} = $words{$word} +1;. Even if no key and counter associated with the word form exist, this will still work because perl will simply create the appropriate key and set its counter to 1, which is actually quite an ingenious way of achieving the task. The technical term for this is autovivification because the variable in question 'automatically springs to life' (cf. Wall et al. 2000: 254).

As we now only store each word form we encounter only once and then simply increase the frequency value associated with it, we can save a fair amount of memory and processing effort, since (1) there is only ever a single word form *entry* or *type* to store, and (2) we avoid the cost of sorting a potentially very large number of items before we can even eliminate any redundant items.

9.4 SORTING AND PRINTING THE LIST

Now that we have seen how easy it is to create the frequency list itself, it only becomes slightly more complicated to produce the right type of output because we need to pay proper attention to what our *sort key(s)* is/are going to be and how we are actually going to specify which items are to be compared. Furthermore, we also need to understand how we can specify multiple sort keys, but luckily for us this is quite a simple matter because our conditions can simply be 'orred' together, that is, by specifying all alternatives in a row, each one separated from the next by a double pipe (||).

Let us start by finding out how to sort according to the words, that is, the *hash keys*. As before, when we sorted our array, we will obviously make use of the sort function, only that this time we do not (implicitly) iterate over the index positions of an array but over the keys of the hash, which we obtain by using the keys function. However, because hashes are internally neither ordered alphabetically nor even in the order that the keys were created, we still have to rely on the sort function and its associated auxiliary variables $a and $b to list the keys in their appropriate order, which is done by chaining the functions and their respective arguments together, as in the following code snippet: foreach $word (sort { $a cmp $b } keys %words) { ... }. Now, as before, if we want to reverse the order to output the words from z to A, we would simply reverse $a and $b.

In order to sort according to the values, we do something very similar, only that this time, we specify the sorting according to the values associated with the hash keys, also using numerical comparison, as in: `foreach $word (sort { $words{ $a} <=> $words{$b} } keys %words) { ... }.`

The most sensible form a frequency list might take is usually a list sorted according to the frequency values in descending order, in other words starting with the words that have the highest frequency. This can easily be achieved by using the code from immediately above and reversing the order of $a and $b, but theoretically this does not guarantee that our keys (words) also get sorted in the right order, which is what we would definitely want as a secondary sort key. In order to accomplish this, we need to specify our alternative by appending it after the numerically descending sort within the sorting block like this: `foreach $word (sort { $words{$b} <=> $words{$a} || $a cmp $b } keys %words) {...}.` **[Exercise 29]** To practise creating frequency lists and this type of sorting, let us do another exercise where we rewrite 'simple_vocab.pl' as 'freq_list.pl', eliminating the redundant arrays and replacing the @words array by the %words hash. You should be able to reuse the file processing/cleanup routine from before. Furthermore, we will make a few more adjustments to the program to allow us to use the program to create either sorted vocabulary lists or proper frequency lists. To do this:

1. Make the first argument to the program an indicator (flag) to indicate the type of list, either -*l* for 'list' or -*f* for 'frequency list'.
2. Adjust the program to generate an output filename from the input filename automatically. The name of the output filename should be the same as for the original file, but the extension should be either *lst*, to indicate a vocabulary list, or *frq*, to indicate a frequency list.
3. Depending on the flag, the final loop that outputs the list should either produce the vocabulary list or an appropriately sorted frequency list and write this to the relevant output file.
4. Do not forget to test the results on a few different files to see whether you have specified the right sorting order and whether the output file names have been generated correctly.

Being able to create word or word frequency lists is one of the most essential types of functionality required in *corpus/computational linguistics* or *natural language engineering/processing* because it provides the basis for document classification or indexing, domain identification, and many other purposes. On a less technical level, though, it may also be extremely useful for language teachers or students who want to be able to extract specific vocabulary lists of the most relevant words in a given textual domain for vocabulary practice or self-study.

## 10

MORE REPETITIVENESS OR HOW TO TIE THINGS TOGETHER (INTRODUCING MODULARITY)

When we began writing slightly more complex programs in the previous chapters, hopefully you will have noticed that we frequently encountered specific programming tasks that needed to be executed repeatedly within one and the same program or across programs, which introduced a certain degree of redundancy. Recoding the same or at least very similar code all the time – even if we use cut and paste – is a rather tedious exercise, so we would like to avoid this as much as possible. Furthermore, the longer our programs get because of repeating similar bits of code in this way, the more unwieldy and difficult they become to understand. This is exactly the point where we need to start thinking about adding a bit of *modularity* to our programs in order to save ourselves this trouble. Modularity essentially means that we structure and code our programs in such a way that we identify and 'extract' repetitive tasks and make sure that we only need to write the corresponding routines once, but can reuse them as often as we like, either within one and the same program or by importing them into different programs.

For example, if we needed to convert a corpus into a specific format for processing it with a special program, we would probably have one main program that creates a list of files in a given folder, then iterates over all these files, converting them one by one and writes them to a different folder. The conversion task, although it could also be embedded in the main program, is an ideal task for a subroutine – a kind of small sub-program – that we would call from within the main body of the program whenever we need to process a new file. In this way, we keep the main program simpler and easier to read, and can also modify it more easily if we later need to add a different bit of functionality, such as changing the output folder if we encounter a file with a given filename prefix and so on.

10.1 FUNCTIONS AND SUBROUTINES

As we shall see in this chapter, there a different levels of modularity. At the lowest level, we encounter functions and subroutines. In other programming languages (such as Microsoft Visual Basic™), a *function* is usually a piece of code that somehow computes and returns a value, whereas a *subroutine* or *procedure* is a routine that simply performs a series of actions without returning a value. In Perl, there is actually no such distinction or restriction, but we normally refer to built-in routines as functions, whereas any routine that is *user-defined* is generally called a *subroutine*. We have already used a number of different functions, such as print, chomp, substr, open, close, die, sort, plus a few more, and seen that they usually take one or more arguments and at least some of them return an obvious value or even a list of values. We will now take a look at how we can achieve similar things in our own subroutines.

10.1.1 CREATING YOUR OWN SUBROUTINES

When discussing subroutines, we need to distinguish between their *definitions* and ways of calling them from within a program. Subroutine definitions look a little similar to the kind of blocks that we have seen for the various types of loops because their main bits of code are in fact enclosed in the same kind of paired curly brackets. However, the main formal difference between them and loops is that, rather than having a condition preceding the curly brackets, we have the keyword sub, followed by the name of the subroutine. As the subroutine is user-defined, whenever you create one you obviously get to pick its name, too, so – as with variable names – you have the chance of using something meaningful and mnemonic, preferably something that clearly reflects its functionality. Thus, if you had two subroutines that were to help you to identify items in a frequency list that occur with the highest or lowest frequency (provided that there are actually such unique items), you would probably want to call them something like (sub) get_max_freq and (sub) get_min_freq, respectively. For an in-depth discussions of good and sensible practice in naming subroutines, take a look at Conway 2005.

Inside the subroutine body, you then get to specify which arguments – if any – it takes, which type(s) of actions you want it to perform and whether you want it to produce one or more values, too. If the subroutine is to produce such values, the result is usually transferred by prefixing the variable(s) to be sent back to the *caller* by the return keyword, which also marks the final statement of the subroutine. If not, the value of the last expression evaluated is automatically returned.

Having dealt with the background theory, we can now start writing our very first subroutine, a rather basic form of *dictionary lookup* that will allow us to perform some (simple-minded) automatic word-for-word translation from English to German, where we use a hash to store the *translation equivalents* in both languages. The English word will be our key, and the subroutine only needs to look up this key and to return the German equivalent. For the sake of simplicity, we assume that we have already defined the dictionary hash as part of the main program code and called it %dict. Now, our subroutine is still going to need an argument to be passed to it, which will of course be the English word. It will get this from the arguments array @_ that is implicitly passed to any subroutine or function. As with the @ARGV array for the main program, we can retrieve items from @_ by using the shift operator. The return value of our subroutine would then obviously have to be the value associated with the hash key represented by the English word, so that our subroutine could look like this:

```
1  sub dictionary_lookup {
2      # retrieve a single argument from the @_ array
3      $word = shift;
```

```
4        # look up the word
5        $equivalent = $dict{$word};
6        # 'send' the translation equivalent back to the
         main program
7        return $equivalent;
8    }
```

We could even have left out the `return` statement in line 7, but it is better pro-gramming practice always to make the return values of your subroutines explicit. Please also note that we have declared and initialised two (potentially) new vari-ables, `$word` and `$equivalent`, in our subroutine. Now, as the subroutine in our case is in fact longer than the piece of code we would normally require to look up a word in the `%dict` hash, this may look like a bit of overkill, but there are still some distinct advantages in using a subroutine approach. The first one is that it is easier to identify what the program does whenever it performs the lookup (provided that we have given it a telling name), simply because it is quicker and easier to read the single subroutine name in the later subroutine call, rather than having to try and understand what happens in the assignment `$equivalent = $dict{$word};`. The next one is that, as the subroutine may get longer and more complex, it will eventually save us some typing effort after all. And finally, if the nature of our data should ever require a different processing approach, we can just change the subroutine (and potentially the associated data structure) and have this change automatically reflected in all parts of our program that make use of the subroutine, rather than having to rewrite all the passages where we make use of its functionality. In our concrete case, you may have noticed that the subroutine in its present form only returns something meaningful if the English word does indeed occur in the dictionary. However, if it does not, we may want to provide the user with an indication that we cannot find a translation equivalent in our dictionary, for example by returning a string containing three question marks (`'???'`).

10.1.2 CALLING A SUBROUTINE

Invoking or calling a subroutine is generally done by using its name, prefixed by an ampersand (`&`) symbol and followed by its argument list in brackets, for example, `&dictionary_lookup($word)`. Even though there is an alternative way, we will not discuss this here, since it is potentially error prone. This notation by prefixing the ampersand to the subroutine also makes it look like we are referring to it as if it were a variable, which is actually something we can do, but this is a topic that is too advanced for this course.

Let us now try using our subroutine in a real program that we will call 'simple_translator.pl' and which will allow us to 'translate' from English to German.

1. Insert the subroutine from above at the end of your program.
2. Declare a hash variable `%dict` and initialise it to contain the key-value pairs: *there/dort, is/ist, a/ein, linguist/Sprachwissenschaftler*.

3. Declare a variable `$sentence` and initialise it to *there is a linguist*.
4. Set up a `foreach` loop to iterate over each `$word` returned by the `split` function, with a space as delimiter and the sentence as its second argument, in other words `foreach $word (split / /, $sentence) {...}`.
5. Inside the loop body, pass each word to the subroutine and add/concatenate the return value, followed by a space, to `$translation`, thus building up the translation step by step.
6. Since we have now added an extra space to the end of the concatenated translation string, remove this by using the `substr` function.
7. Create some descriptive output to show the original sentence and its translation.
8. Test the program.

When evaluating the result of our translation program, we can see that this already works quite well for our particular example, even though there are some obvious problems a real-life translation program would still have to cope with, including issues of:

- idiomaticity (*there is* may also be translated into German as *es gibt*, rather than *dort ist*)
- as well as of gender-related polysemy (*linguist* in English is ambiguous as to its gender, thus making our simplified translation unintentionally sexist because we are automatically using the masculine equivalent *Sprachwissenschaftler* in German)
- and the need for its related morphological/morphosyntactic adjustment in German for a female linguist (that is *a* ⇒ *eine* and *linguist* ⇒ *Sprachwissenschaftlerin*)

Of course, similar problems do exist in other languages, at least those that distinguish gender morphologically or in some other way, but you would not have expected automatic translation to be such an easy job now, anyway, would you?

10.1.3 LOCALISING VARIABLES AND BEING STRICT WITH YOURSELF

Apart from the linguistic problems discussed immediately above, there are also some potential further problems with our existing program, related to two very important issues we need to introduce at this point. These are variable *scope* and how to enforce the declaration of variables. Understanding about these will make your life as a programmer considerably easier and help you to trap potential errors before they may arise in the first place.

So far, any variable that we have created in one of our programs has always been globally accessible from anywhere within the program. Because we have only been writing comparatively small and non-modular programs, this has not caused any naming conflicts. However, when you start writing programs that split up the individual tasks into different modules, you may inadvertently find yourself using the same variable name – for example, something like `$word` – twice, which may have unintended, but nasty, side-effects. [**Exercise 30**] We will first try to demonstrate this by modifying the previous program a little and will then discuss ways of making the program safer.

1. Copy the previous program to 'simple_translator_buggy.pl'.
2. Modify the `foreach` loop to include an additional statement after the concatenation of the translation, where you append the value of $word, plus an additional space, to $original in the same way that you concatenated the previous translation.
3. After the loop, also strip the additional whitespace off $original.
4. Modify the final output, adding a newline, followed by the value of $original, a space and three question marks.
5. Last, inside the subroutine, add a statement before returning the value of $equivalent, where you assign $equivalent to $word.

Now, when you test this new version, you might be in for a surprise because you would normally expect $original to hold a copy of the original sentence. However, as we reassigned to it inside the subroutine, the value it used to have in the main body of the program was in fact changed by the subroutine and is forever lost. In our case, this is a constructed example of what might go wrong if you only use *global* variables, but in real-life programs that may often run into hundreds of lines of code or be made up of individual modules, problems like this can easily arise and the source of the error might be very difficult to identify and fix.

Luckily, there is a simple solution to repairing this, which is to use *localised* variables whenever possible, and only use global ones if you explicitly decide that you need them in order to share data between different routines or modules. In Perl, you localise a variable by prefixing it with the keyword my. [**Exercise 31**] To see how this will fix our previous problem, simply add this before $word in the first line inside the `dictionary_lookup` subroutine and run the program again. This time, the contents that end up in $original should indeed be reflected as the original sentence in the output because the variable $word *inside* the subroutine is now different from the variable by the same name *outside* the subroutine in the main part of the program. And thus, the latter is not affected by the assignment to $word in the penultimate line of the subroutine block.

Perl also provides a way for you to enforce the discipline of localising your variables for you. This is achieved by adding the statement use strict; before the beginning of the main part of your program. The use keyword provides a way of *importing* external modules (and variables) into your programs, something we shall learn more about in the next section. Making use of this feature may also prevent you from accidentally using a variable name that contains a typo because the strict module will automatically report any undeclared variables in your program and never allow it to run in the first place. Of course, one thing it will not prevent you from is to declare a variable at the beginning of your code and then not localising it inside a subroutine, which could again cause the same problem we had before. As a further safety measure, you can also switch on *warnings* about a variety of different errors, such as redeclaration of variables or unused variables and so forth by adding the -w switch to the end of the shebang line.

As a final exercise in this section, add use strict; to the beginning of your program, and then observe the error messages you will get and try to fix them by localising your variables appropriately. Appropriately in this case means that you should define globally accessible variables that are to be used by the whole program once, preferably at the beginning of the program and variables that are supposed to be local to a subroutine or other type of block once at the beginning of the relevant block, or at least before its first use within the block. Of course, from now on, you should always make use of the features described above in all your programs.

10.2 REFERENCES AND MODULES

With modules, you can – quite literally – take the concept of modularity one step further than we have done before in using subroutines. They often even comprise whole *libraries* of subroutines or processing mechanisms that you write once and then use many times in different types of applications. Let us assume, for example, that you regularly need to process HTML files in your work, but you obviously only want to process the text contained on the pages and simply ignore the HTML markup. In order to accomplish this, you could write a module that will allow you to strip out the HTML code and write the data either to a file or an appropriate data structure, such as an array of lines, which you can then pass to your main program and process as if you had read in an ordinary plain text file.

Alternatively, you may actually need to distinguish between different types of information on the page, such as the text contained in headings versus ordinary paragraphs. In this case, you would probably want your module to create a hash for you, where you use one key for all headings and another for the paragraphs, storing all headings in an array associated with the headings key and all paragraphs in the corresponding paragraphs array. We will write such a (simplified) module later on, once we have taken a closer look at how modules are formally distinguished from ordinary Perl programs. Before doing so, though, we need to introduce another important feature of Perl called *references*, which allow us to create complex, as well as often *anonymous*, data structures.

10.2.1 BASIC NAMED REFERENCES

References in Perl are similar to *pointers* in other programming languages like C or C++. They allow us to refer to the contents of a particular variable or *memory location*. References are often stored in scalar variables, but may frequently also be associated with hash keys. To create a reference to a non-anonymous variable or sub-routine, you prefix the variable/subroutine by a backslash and assign it to a scalar variable like this: $words_array_ref = \@words;. The syntax we just used would then allow us to refer to the contents of @words via its reference $words_array_ref, provided we *dereference* it properly again, which we shall learn about shortly. You may now be wondering why this is useful at all, so I will give you a concrete example of where this might be of potential relevance. Imagine a subroutine, like the one we used for our translation program, but which returns the translation equivalents for a long array of words instead of a single one. Now, as we learnt before, all the arguments to a subroutine are passed to it via the @_ array, so, if we were to pass our @words array to it, we would actually be copying all the values of the original array before using them. Instead, though, we can simply pass our reference $words_array_ref to it, which means that we avoid copying all the words, only passing a single variable to the subroutine, which will then allow the subroutine to access all the elements in @words through the reference to its location in memory. This not only saves memory but also a little bit of execution time, as the copying would obviously not be instantaneous, either.

Being able to pass an array reference to a subroutine is by no means the only use for references, though. As we shall see later, they also provide the means for creating and accessing Perl objects, as well as *tying* the contents of text entry boxes to variables in a GUI and so forth. To dereference a reference again, we need to know what type of data is stored inside it, and then prefix the reference by the appropriate symbol.

Thus, to gain access to all the 'contents' of $words_array_ref inside a foreach loop, we could write foreach my $word (@$words_array_ ref) {...}, to iterate over the keys in a hash reference $words_hash_ref, foreach my $word (sort keys %$words_hash_ref) {...}, and to retrieve the contents of the scalar reference $word_ref, we would use $$word_ ref. If you want to be even more explicit, you can enclose the reference in curly brackets and then prefix the appropriate symbol, for instance @{$words_array_ ref}. This may soon become necessary, anyway, once you start using more deeply *nested* data structures.

More or less the same rules as for retrieving single elements from arrays or hashes apply to accessing parts of referenced multi-element data structures. Here, too, the symbol to be used for dereferencing a single item inside them is $. Dereferencing a single element of an array reference does not require any particularly difficult syntax and thus $$words_array_ref[0] or ${$words_array_ref}[0] would allow you to work with the first element of the @words array, while accessing the key this through the reference to the %words hash would require you to write $$words_hash_ref{'this'} or ${$words_hash_ref}{'this'}.

As this looks quite complicated and maybe even a bit confusing, there are also two simpler alternative variants, which simply make use of the reference, followed by an -> arrow, and either the array index or hash key. This would allow us to rewrite the previous examples as $words_array_ref->[0] and $words_hash_ref ->{'this'}, respectively.

The more deeply nested your data structures get, the more complex your dereferencing may appear, which may be daunting to you, apart from providing many potential sources of error. Nevertheless, the more practice you get in using references, the easier it will become for you to use them efficiently and correctly, so do not despair too quickly!

10.2.2 ANONYMOUS REFERENCES

All the references we looked at above were references to named items, in other words, specifically declared individual arrays and hashes. However, for some types of more complex data structures, it is not convenient to declare each single element explicitly, just as you would not normally want to have to give a specific name to each single element of an array. Let us take the example of a proper monolingual dictionary, something more elaborate than our simple one that just contained translation equivalents. Here, the data structure would generally consist of an *entry*, where each entry has a number of features that are associated with a *headword* or *lemma*, such as its part(s)-of-speech (PoS), phonetic transcription, a definition, plus a number of suitable examples and so forth. Often, there may even be multiple numbered sub-entries for the different meanings, which would then potentially in turn have the same feature entries associated with them. The data structure that would suggest itself for the simplest form of dictionary – the one without multiple sub-entries per headword – would therefore be a hash, where all the entries are associated with headwords that serve as the (top-level) hash keys. The features associated with each entry would then most likely consist of another hash, where each feature label would serve as the key, for example, 'pos' for part-of-speech information, 'pron' for pronunciation, 'def' for the definition and 'ex' for the examples. Now, all of these features might potentially take on multiple values, too, because words can be *grammatically polysemous* (*book* as noun or verb), have multiple pronunciations ([aɪðə] versus [iːðə]) and so on, so that we would probably want to store this information inside an array if necessary. We could of course compute unique hash keys for each of our sub-hashes, as well as the arrays, to set them up and through which to access them again later on. However, would it not be so much nicer if we could simply refer to the same keys, but for different words, each time we wanted to deal with a particular type of information? Well, Perl does make this possible via references to anonymous data structures.

To set up an anonymous data array or a hash, you basically only need to learn about some minor differences in the way that they are declared/initialised in contrast to their named counterparts. Let us start with the basic syntax before we explore how to specify more complex data structures in one go.

To set up a reference to an anonymous array and store it in $anon_array_ref, we would use square brackets instead of the round ones used for named arrays, thus yielding $anon_array_ref = []; to set up an empty anonymous array. To create the hash counterpart, you say $anon_hash_ref = {}; because the curly brackets allow us to declare anonymous hashes. To store some information in our dictionary %dict pertaining to the word *house*, as well as other words not fully shown here, we could write:

```
1   %dict = (
2     house => {
3       pos => [qw (NN V)],
4       pron => [qw (haʊs haʊz)],
5       def => ['A type of building that people live
          in.','The act of  accommodating s.o. inside a
          house.'],
```

```
6     ex => ['My friends recently bought a very nice
      house in the countryside.','The refugee camp
      houses people from many different countries
      around the world.'],
7   },
8   castle => {
9     ...
10  },
11  );
```

The qw (quote word) operator used above provides a convenient mechanism for specifying a list of whitespace separated items efficiently, without having to quote each individual item or using a comma between the list items.

To access the features of a particular entry, we could then write a subroutine that expects two arguments, a headword and a feature. Let us assume – for the sake of simplicity – that we would always want to output all the information related to a particular word feature. As we may need to distinguish between single value feature entries and those that come in the shape of an array, however, we would still need to find a mechanism for doing so and handling the two cases separately. How we do this by using the ref operator is shown in the following subroutine.

```
1   sub get_property {
2       my ($word, $property) = @_;
3       my $ref_type = ref $dict{$word}{$property};
4       if ($ref_type eq 'ARRAY') {
5          my $num = 0;
6          my $property_string = '';
7          foreach my $prop_element (@{$dict{$word}
           {$property}}) {
8              $num++;
9              $property_string .= $num."\t".
               $prop_element."\n";
10         }
11         chomp $property_string;
12         return $property_string;
13         }
14      else {
15         return $dict{$word}{$property};
16         }
17  }
```

In line 3 above, we first use the ref operator to determine the type of reference for the property as we could potentially store either a scalar or an anonymous array in the reference, depending on whether we have single or multiple values. If the property of the feature is a single scalar, we can just return this (lines 14–16), but if we find an array, we certainly want to produce some nicer output to distinguish the individual elements (lines 4–13). For this purpose, we build up a property string where each element that is retrieved from the array and added to the string is prefixed by a number and a tab, as well as separated from the next element via a newline.

[**Exercise 32**] As an exercise, let us now put the two samples from above together into a program called 'sample_dict.pl'. This program should accept a headword and a feature/property name from the command line, look up the property value(s), and write them out to a file called 'dict_test.txt' in the current directory. Make sure you add some appropriate error handling at the beginning of the program to guarantee that the user provides at least two values. Also think about where you might need to introduce some more error handling to ensure that the program will always return some appropriate output or else inform the user that this is not possible. The sample solution provided by me only contains entries for the two words *house* and *castle*, but for your own program you should also (minimally) add some further entries for *fortress, car, bicycle, bus* and *train*, always paying attention to cases of possible semantic and grammatical polysemy which may result in the need for setting up anonymous arrays.

Of course, despite mimicking an already fairly useful dictionary structure, the above program is still only a toy program. In order to turn it into a fully fledged dictionary utility, we would at least want to be able to provide some interface(s) for reading in and building up the dictionary information from external sources, returning the information we can retrieve from the dictionary in various different formats for different types of programs that may need to make use of it, as well as probably designing a GUI for performing some basic actions, such as visualising the result of the lookup we are currently rather inconveniently outputting to a file to be able to deal with the phonetic information. In order to accomplish these things, we would most certainly at least want to turn parts of this extended program into modules, which is the topic we return to now.

10.2.3 WHAT DO MODULES LOOK LIKE?

The first obvious difference that modules have in comparison with our previous programs is that they usually have the extension *.pm*, rather than *.pl*. The convention is also to make their names start with a capital letter (Wall et al. 2000: 605–6). Even if your operating system or setup routine of your particular Perl distribution may associate the *.pl* extension to be executed automatically for you, this is rarely the case for *.pm* files. You can nevertheless execute modules in the same way as other programs by explicitly invoking the interpreter on the command line, saying 'perl My_module.pm', provided that it actually makes sense to run the module like an ordinary program, which will certainly not always be the case.

The next difference is that Perl modules should always start with a `package` statement before any other modules are *imported* or any module-specific parameters *exported*. The package name has to be identical to the name of the module, but usually excludes the *.pm* extension.

Next, we need to make sure that we can in fact offer the functionality our module is supposed to provide to other perl programs or modules, which is done by specifying a means of exporting as much of this functionality as necessary. In order to implement this, we add the following lines to any non-object-oriented module after the `package` statement.

```
use Exporter;
our @ISA = qw (Exporter);
our @EXPORT = qw (list of items to be exported);
```

In line 1, we first import the `Exporter` module that allow us to export things in the first place. The second line defines a globally accessible, but package-specific, array that specifies from which other package(s) our package inherits features. This is actually one of the advanced object-oriented features that we do not want to discuss in detail in this book. Suffice it to say at this point that it allows our package to claim that it is also an `Exporter` and therefore to use any of the functionality that the `Exporter` module provides if no appropriate subroutines are found within the package itself. Also note the semantic similarity between the keywords my and our in this context, which should make their functionality immediately obvious to anyone who is a little linguistically minded. The name of the array (`@ISA`) is another feature that Perl has adopted from semantic theory, where 'is a' expresses a *hyponymy* relationship, for example, as in 'a house is a building' and so on. Line 3 is used to specify an array of variables or subroutines that should be made accessible automatically to any program using the module.

And last, but not least, every module has to be terminated by a `1;`. This signals to the importing programs that the module has been read in completely and successfully.

10.2.4 IMPORTING AND USING MODULES

As we have seen previously, modules are imported into the *namespaces* of other programs by means of use statements. This is very easy and works well if you are using modules that can be found in the standard Perl installation directories, other Perl libraries that are in the Perl path or, as we will design them, are located inside the same directory as our main program. It does, however, get a little more complicated and less flexible when you start producing and importing modules that are located in different levels of sub-directories, but this is something we will not discuss in this book as it is a more advanced topic.

There are also two more aspects we have not mentioned so far. One is that the package name of the module to be used can also be followed by a specification of only particular bits of functionality to be provided by it, rather than automatically loading everything the module exports. This is again done by using the qw operator and specifying a list of everything you want to import. The other thing is that, in Perl, unlike in other languages that make a distinction between *public* and *private* variables, all elements of a package can be accessed, even if none of them are exported.

This is always possible by prefixing the appropriate variable or subroutine by its *fully qualified* package name, as in, for example $My_module::string, if we had a module called My_module.pm and a variable $string defined inside it that we wanted to access. Please note that the prefix that indicates the type of variable occurs at the beginning of the fully qualified name and not the variable name itself. If you have imported the module functionality though, you can simply use the name of the variable or subroutine as if it were part of your importing program, provided that the variable/subroutine name is not ambiguous.

10.2.5 WRITING A SIMPLISTIC HTML PAGE DOWNLOADER AND PARSER

As an exercise, we will now make use of many of the things we have previously learnt and put them together to write our very own module that will allow us to download an HTML page from the Internet, store a local copy and parse it to extract some text from it. Please bear in mind, though, that this is only intended as an exercise to help you understand and design modules because the functionality we can achieve here will again be limited, although you will of course be able to expand it later yourself. If you ever need to process data that you know may be 'ill-formed' in some way or might contain more complex HTML elements, such as tables, you should use a ready made Perl module, such as HTML::Parser or HTML::TokeParser, which are already integrated into most current Perl distributions or can otherwise be downloaded from CPAN.

Let us start with the global specifications of your task. Our module is supposed to allow us to connect to a server on the web, request a web page from it and store its contents on our disk. To be able to do this, we will make use of a module called LWP::Simple, which is hopefully already installed on your system. If not, you need to download the LWP suite of modules which contains it, and use one of the methods discussed earlier to install it on your computer. The LWP (Library for World Wide Web in Perl; cf. Burke 2002: 1) suite, of which Simple is a sub-module, comprises a number of modules that allow you to interact with web servers in various ways for downloading or submitting different types of information, which makes it possible to design fairly complex tools that even enable you to *mirror* or *crawl* whole websites. The functionality we will employ in our exercise is actually only a tiny part of what you can do with it, but nevertheless something that allows you to exploit the WWW as a huge corpus.

Once we have downloaded a web page, we obviously also want to be able to process it in some way. To discuss one of the predefined parser modules here would take up too much time and space, so we will slurp in the file and provide some *handler* subroutines that will help us to extract headings and paragraphs from the HTML. If you want to learn more about parsing and working with web pages in Perl, I would suggest you read Sean Burke's *Perl and LWP*.

In order to demonstrate how to use LWP::Simple for our purposes, I will give you an example of what the subroutine that is used to download the page could look like. You can later test this on a sample web page from the website accompanying this book that contains some relatively basic HTML. This page is called 'sample_page.html' and you can access it directly at <http://www.euppublishing.com/page/essential_prog_linguistics/sample_page.html>.

```
1   sub fetch_page {
2     my $url = shift;
3     my $local_file = $url;
4     for ($local_file) {
5       s|^\w+?:/+||x;
6       # remove any trailing slashes
7       s|/$||;
8       s|/|__|g;
9     }
10    # add html if no extension present or other than
      html
11    if ($local_file !~ /html?$/) {
12      $local_file = $local_file.'.html';
13    }
14    # create directory for downloads or abort
15    if (!-e './downloads') {
16      mkdir './downloads' or die "unable to create
        downloads directory!";
17    }
18    $local_file = './downloads/'.$local_file;
19    # attempt to get the page
20    my $download_status = getstore($url,
      $local_file);
21    # inform us as to whether the download was
      possible...
22    if (is_success($download_status)) {
23    print "OK";
24        }
25    # ... or not
26    else {
27      warn "Download for $url failed. Error number:
        ", $download_status,"\n";
28    }
29  }
```

As far as the particular programming constructs used are concerned, the subroutine shown above should not be too difficult to understand, but I will still explain a few points that may be unclear to you if you are not very familiar with web conventions or some of the features of LWP::Simple. Let us begin with the way we generate a local file name from the web address (*URL; Uniform Resource Locator*) of the page we are going to fetch. This involves all the lines from 3 to 13. First, in line 3, we make a copy of the original web address and manipulate this in order to make it usable as a filename for local storage. Much of this happens in the substitutions from lines 5 to 8 and is necessary because URLs consist of Unix-style path names that we do not want to replicate in our filename because we do not want to have to set up the same directory structure as on the web server, just for getting a single file. This, of course, would be different if we wanted to mirror a whole website. In line 5, we first remove the web protocol 'prefix', which will probably be 'http://' in most cases, but could occasionally be different. Next, if we have a web address that should happen to end in a slash, rather than a web page extension, we remove this (line 7) and replace all remaining path separators by a double underscore, to be able to distinguish them from any potential single underscores that may be part of the original path structure. In lines 11–13, we ensure that all page names that do not end in *htm* or *html*, such as maybe php script-generated pages or index pages (remember the final slash), do receive an *html* extension, so that we can handle them all in the same way, including opening them directly from within our *file manager* for inspection. Please note that I have here chosen pipe symbols as the delimiters for all substitutions, too, as this saves us from having to escape the slashes that are likely to occur frequently in URLs.

In lines 14–18, we first check to see whether a *downloads* directory exists and, if not, attempt to create it. If we cannot create one, we abort the program because we do not seem to have write permissions, anyway. If we are successful, though, or if the directory already exists, we modify the local filename again to include the path to this directory.

The remainder of the subroutine does the actual work, using the `getstore` routine from `LWP::Simple` with the download URL and the local filename as arguments. Because we cannot be sure that our download is definitely going to succeed, we store the return value of this routine in `$download_status`. We then use the `LWP is_success` function to check this and either print out a success message or output the download status – together with an indication of the URL we failed to get – as a warning. The final newline is simply used to suppress the information pertaining to perl's default error output telling us where in our program the error occurred.

[**Exercise 33**] Now, create a new module called 'Html_handler.pm' and copy the `fetch_page` subroutine into it. Also make sure that you add all the statements required for exporting this routine, and so on, at the top of the program. Once you have done so, follow the instructions below to set up a few more subroutines that will allow us to extract headings and paragraphs – or any other elements that we might choose to extract later – from an HTML page and store them in a hash of arrays that we can then return to a calling program.

1. Set up a localised hash called `%page_elements` and initialise the two keys 'headings' and 'paragraphs' to two empty anonymous arrays.
2. Set up a localised scalar variable called `$file_contents` to hold the contents of any web page we read in.

In the next step, we want to set up a subroutine that slurps in the file contents, but because we do not know its encoding beforehand and want to be able to handle all characters correctly – if possible – we first attempt to retrieve the encoding information from the page, provided that the author has indeed specified it. If it is contained in the HTML, it will be stored in a `<meta>` element inside the header, which will look like this if the page has been encoded in UTF-8: `<meta http-equiv="Content-Type" content="text/html; charset=utf-8" />`. We therefore open the page in UTF-8 first and then try to match and store the `charset` information. This should be possible because the meta `content` information should only contain predefined characters that occur in the ASCII range. In the next step, we can then – if necessary – reopen the file in the specified encoding for reading and later output it in UTF-8. Once we have extracted the encoding information, we interpolate this into the `encoding` part of the `open` function or abort the file reading process if there is an error, due to Perl perhaps being unable to deal with this particular encoding.

3. Now, create a subroutine called 'read_page' that accepts a file name argument, opens the corresponding HTML file and stores its contents in `$file_contents`. Once you have extracted the `charset` information, though, use the `lc` function before comparing it to our default encoding and possibly interpolating it into the `open` function.

Next, we need to create the two subroutines that will extract the heading and paragraph texts. To get the contents of both headings and paragraphs, we can use a `while` loop and global matching operation, together with some backreferences that will help us to match paired start and end tags, as well as to capture the content in between them. This is a little similar to the way we replaced HTML tags in 'substitute_html.pl', but still sufficiently different to merit some extra explanation because, this time, we are not just replacing complete tags and because we also want to anticipate some ill-formed HTML that may contain artificial line breaks inside tags or their contents. To be able to match newlines along with other content, we need to make use of the `s` modifier. The first set of capturing brackets here needs to be set up around the element name and re-used as `\1` later to match the end tag of the element. As there is a fair chance that the start tag may also contain some attributes, we need to specify that they might optionally be present before the closing angled bracket, so we can set up a non-greedy, non-capturing, optional match that will match any character but the closing angled bracket. Anything between the closing angled bracket of the start tag and the end tag can then be captured in the next set of brackets, again using a non-greedy quantifier. This will then obviously be stored in `$2`.

4. Knowing this, you can now write the two subroutines called 'extract_headings' and 'extract_paragraphs', where you `push` the contents of `$2` onto the end of the 'headings' and 'paragraphs' arrays inside `%page_contents`. If you are unsure about how to do this, I would suggest you reread our discussion of references (p. 104) before consulting my sample solution.

5. As the contents we extract using the two subroutines may in turn contain nested elements, set up another subroutine called 'clean_element_contents' that takes a string and removes all tags from it before returning it.

6. Now, go back to the two extraction routines and modify them to integrate the tag removal before the text is actually stored in the relevant array.
7. Finally, write another subroutine called 'return_elements' that takes the name of a possible key in `%page_contents` and returns the anonymous array associated with it.
8. Once you have finished implementing all the subroutines, make sure you do not forget to add them to the list of items to be exported.

Creating this module will probably be more difficult for you as I am not giving you as many step-by-step instructions as previously. However, by now you should already have reached a slightly advanced stage in your programming career, so, given a bit of time, you ought to be able to handle this task. And if you should end up struggling too much, you can always consult the sample solution.

The above is only part of this exercise, though. When you have finished writing the module, you also need to be able to test it, so:

1. Create a program that uses the module in order to display either all headings or all paragraphs using a `foreach` loop.
2. This program should accept two command line arguments, the type to display and a filename to parse.
3. Test the program on the sample file.

In case you are now wondering why I gave you this exercise and what kind of linguistic merit there is in being able to extract headings and paragraphs separately from a web page, let us think about what kind of information is contained in these specific textual elements and in which way they may affect our processing options for this type of data. In terms of text-linguistic relevance, headings may of course be of special interest in categorising or summarising the contents of a page, just like the headings of newspaper articles give you an idea of their contents and whether they may be interesting to read in the first place. At the same time, regarding the frequency analysis and potential approaches to the analysis of texts based on this, they often in fact contain redundant data because their contents are generally repeated inside the paragraphs associated with them. Therefore, what may have been intended as a help for guiding the reader and structuring the text may, for example, affect the analysis of complexity issues because it might influence such features as *type-token ratios*, which are often seen as essential in calculating complexity. Depending on our attitude towards this problem, we would therefore probably at least want to have the option of either in- or excluding frequency counts of tokens contained in headings.

Since you now know enough about the basics of references and modules, we can continue with a special type of module, the object, in the next chapter.

11

OBJECTS

In this section, we will introduce the basics of object-oriented design in Perl, as a more in-depth treatment of the topic would be too much for an introductory course. Before we learn how to construct and use objects in Perl, however, we first need to discuss a bit of terminology to understand the basic idea behind the concept of object-orientation.

11.1 OO CONCEPTS

Object orientation, as you can also see in the above heading, is often simply abbreviated to *OO*. In OO, an object is a self-contained piece of data that may have particular *properties* and/or *methods* associated with it. A property of an object is essentially a type of variable, such as a scalar, an array or a hash, that stores information pertaining to the object. A method is simply a subroutine that performs a certain type of functionality associated with the object, such as constructing the object or *setting* or *getting* its properties.

Let us take a look at a linguistic example of what could be an object – a verb. A verb may have certain properties associated with it, such as information about whether it is regular or irregular, its tense, number and its person. If it is irregular, then we would probably have to specify all its different potential forms, together with their properties, in other words information about whether the different forms relate to tense forms – for example, *buy, bought, bought* – or person, number and tense – for example, *be, am, are, was*, and so on. Its methods would then provide ways of changing or setting the associated properties, depending on (morpho-) syntactic conditions, such as the need to adjust for subject-verb-agreement, or retrieving such information that has already been stored, via so-called *accessor methods*.

When you write an object, you effectively create a blueprint of that object (called a *class*), but the object itself does not really exist yet until it is *instantiated* because a particular program is actually asking for the object to be created. Creating the object is usually done via a special method of the object, called a *constructor*, which may also initialise some properties that are either deemed to be the default values of the object or may be passed to the constructor as arguments. By convention, the constructor is generally called 'new', but of course you could also call it something more meaningful, such as 'make_verb' if your object is indeed a verb.

11.2 CREATING AN OBJECT IN PERL

Most objects in Perl use hashes as their internal data structure, although it is quite possible to use arrays, too, especially as it is always feasible to nest one data structure inside another. We saw this when we stored arrays inside the hash in our module in the preceding section. Just like a module, an object is also a `package`, so we need to include the *package name* at the top of our object definition. By convention, object names are also often *capitalised*, although you could equally well use a pre- or suffix – such as 'obj_' or '_obj' – in order to show that whatever we will be creating and using from within another program later is an object, rather than a basic module. The important things in naming the object are – again – only that the name be somewhat explicit and that the filename correspond to whatever you have called the package.

Next, we need to add a constructor for our object, that is, a routine that will create and possibly initialise it, too. The first thing an object needs to know about itself is to which class it belongs, so this is always passed as the first argument to any constructor, and usually stored in a variable called `$class`. As we have just said, objects can be made up of different data types, but no matter which kind of data type you use, the object is usually stored as a reference to an anonymous data structure, which, again by convention, is normally called `$self`.

Apart from setting up the reference to `$self`, you can also use the constructor to initialise various values passed as arguments to the constructor or set as assumed defaults, something we shall take a closer look at shortly when we create a real object. The last two steps we need to perform before we can actually use our object are to `bless` the object into its class and to return the object thus created. The former is achieved simply by using the syntax: `bless $self, $class;`, always assuming of course that you have followed our conventions.

As you can see, designing an object is in fact somewhat easier than creating a basic module because there is no need to specify all the things we had to list for being able to export from our module. The main reason for this is that the properties and methods of objects are usually seen as belonging to the object, so that it is the task of the object itself to *expose* its functionality via appropriate *interfaces*, such as accessor methods. In other words, programs that use objects are generally assumed not to access the object's features themselves but call upon the object to do so.

11.3 CREATING A REGULAR VERB OBJECT

In the following, we will learn how to put theory into practice by constructing an object that will allow us to model regular verbs, such as *count, flush, insist, name, point, watch* and so on. Our object should of course have a constructor that will allow us to create a verb, based on minimally specifying an infinitive form that we will use as a verb *stem*, plus information regarding its *person, tense* and *number*. [**Exercise 34**] We will design the object so that, if no stem is provided, it will call `die` with an appropriate (usage) error message and thereby kill the calling program. Please note, though, that this would not be a very good type of error handling if the object were created as part of a larger program where many different objects are created, even though creating an 'empty' object in any program would most certainly cause *runtime* problems.

Since there is not much we can do with a bare infinitive, we will make sure that our constructor will provide some defaults for person, tense and number, in case these have not been specified by the calling program as arguments to the constructor. We will simply assume that it makes sense to use *1* (that is 1st) as the default for *person*, **present** as the one for *tense*, and **singular** for *number*. For later constructing verb forms from our object(s), we will allow the following possible values for:

- person: 1, 2, 3
- tense: present, pres. part., past, past part.
- number: singular, plural

As we have a number of named string arguments, the data structure for our verb object will be a simple hash, which – in itself – is relatively easy to construct. However, the somewhat tricky thing in our case is that we want to be able to extract the hash keys from our argument list automatically to set them or, in case not all parameters have been provided, use the defaults. This is why, this time, I shall first show the complete constructor and will then discuss the individual points again, before we will add some more methods as an exercise later.

```
1   sub new {
2   my $class = shift;
3   my %args = @_;
4   my $self = {
5       stem => $args{'stem'},
6       person => $args{'person'} || "1",
7       tense => $args{'tense'} || 'present',
8       number => $args{'number'} || 'singular',
9   };
10  die "usage: stem => <stem> [person => <1|2|3>
    number => <singular|plural> tense =>
    <present|past|past part.|pres. part.>]!\n"
    if (!defined $self->{'stem'});
11  bless $self, $class;
12  return $self;
13  }
```

As you can see in line 1, our constructor is conventionally called 'new' and the first argument passed to it is stored in $class. Next, we interpolate all remaining arguments into a hash called %args. This works because, when reading the array into the hash, each array index/position with an even number (including the 0) is used as a key and each following index (with an odd number) as its value. This provides us with a very elegant means of reading in hashes of named arguments for use with objects or subroutines.

In lines 4–9, we create a reference to an anonymous hash and store it in the string variable $self. Inside the hash, we initialise our keys by retrieving the corresponding values from the arguments hash. If the arguments hash does not contain the keys, we set our defaults for person, tense and number, which is achieved via the or (||) operator, just as we did for our sorting routines when specifying alternative sorting criteria. Please also note the final comma in line 8, which is in fact redundant and treated by the interpreter as such. Perl programmers often use this special feature because it makes it easier to remove or move around key-value pairs from hashes without messing up the list and producing program errors.

In the next step, we test to see whether the constructor has been supplied with a value for stem. If not, we use die and print out the appropriate arguments, together with list of their potential values, indicated in angled brackets, where the square brackets indicate optional arguments. In order to test whether a value for stem exists in the hash referenced by $self, we use the defined operator. To dereference the hash in $self and to get to the stem key in its underlying data structure, we use the arrow operator (->) as previously described.

In line 11, we bless our object into its class and return it in line 12. The object blueprint is now finished and we only need to learn how to use it from within another program.

11.4 INSTANTIATING THE VERB OBJECT

Creating an instance of your verb object is a relatively simple matter. Before being able to create a verb object, you first need to import the class definition into the calling program's namespace, which is simply done via the use Verb_obj; statement, as 'Verb_obj' is what we will call our object in this example. If you have not done so yet, you should now copy the constructor from above to a suitably named and 'packaged' file. And, assuming that you have done this correctly, you can now create a new verb object for the verb *count* in another program by saying Verb_obj->new('stem' => 'count');, at the same time making absolutely explicit which property we want to initialise because we are specifying the named argument 'stem' with the corresponding value 'count'.

This would create the object for us, but there is only one small problem with it – we have no way to actually use it! In order to do so, we need to assign our newly created object to a variable that allows us to reference (and dereference) it, so a more sensible way to create the object would be to say something like $verb1 = Verb_obj->new('stem' => 'count');. Instantiating the object in this way would also allow us to see whether the defaults were really set correctly by our constructor, for example, by testing to see whether the number property has automatically been set to 1, using the debugging statement print "person for \$verb1: ", $verb1->{'person'}, "\n";.

All this should work correctly because we know for a fact that our object consists of a hash – rather than any other type of variable – and also that there will definitely be a hash key `person` in our underlying data structure that we can dereference in this way. Just because we can, however, this does not mean that it is the best way to do so, which it definitely is not because we should not force our object users to need to know what the underlying data structure is in order to be able to use our object, especially not if we may ever decide that a different data structure may be more appropriate in future...

11.5 CREATING APPROPRIATE ACCESSOR METHODS

A far better way of allowing the user (or ourselves) to 'interact' with objects and their properties is to provide suitable methods to retrieve these properties or manipulate them. As I said before, these routines, because they allow us to *access* the properties, no matter in which way they are stored, are called *accessor methods*. The simplest forms such methods can take on are so-called *setters* and *getters*, which allow us to *set* or *get* the values associated with the properties. [**Exercise 35**] Since we already know that methods are simply subroutines belonging to an object, it will be easy for us to write these, provided that we bear in mind that they, just like the object, always need to know 'who they belong to', so that the first argument that is passed to them always has to be a reference to the object itself. All remaining arguments in @_ are then 'proper' arguments to the subroutine, as we have seen and used them before.

For simple setters and getters, the only difference between the two is that a getter usually only requires either one or two pieces of information, the object reference, plus optionally the name of the property to retrieve, whereas the setter will additionally need a value to which the property ought to be changed. Now that you know all this, we can write two accessor methods for our verb object, called `get_prop` and `set_prop` respectively, as well as a program that will allow us to test creating objects and getting/setting their properties:

1. Open the previously created verb object package file and add the two accessor methods, each time using appropriately localised variables for the object reference and all remaining parameters. If you want to follow convention, the variable for holding the object reference should probably be called `$self`.
2. For the setter, add a statement that will assign the property argument passed to the method to the corresponding object property.
3. For the getter, simply `return` the value associated with the corresponding value in the object property.
4. Create a new program called 'test_Verb_obj.pl' and import the verb object.
5. Inside the program, create a few verb objects, sometimes using named arguments other than the stem, testing the default values, changing or retrieving the different properties by using the accessor methods and printing them again after having made some changes.

Once you have completed the above exercise, you should be able to appreciate to some extent what the value of objects and their associated accessor methods is, but hopefully you will have also noticed that the functionality we have so far endowed our verbs with is not really terribly useful. In order to turn our verb object into something of more practical use, we will therefore add a new subroutine which will allow us to generate any possible verb form, using either the values we have stored in the properties of the object or named arguments for generating any other regular verbs we could think of, by resorting to the functionality of one and the same object, but without having to produce a new one, thereby making the object an even more powerful linguistic resource.

1. Add a new subroutine called 'make_verbform' to the object definition.
2. Inside the subroutine, use `shift` in order to remove the object reference from `@_` and store it in an appropriate variable.
3. Interpolate the remaining arguments into a hash called `%attributes`, assuming that we are using the same named arguments as for the object itself.
4. Set up a `foreach` loop that iterates over all verb property names, each time checking to see whether the corresponding key exists in `%attributes` and, if not, retrieves the corresponding value from the object itself. This allows us to achieve the dual functionality described above.
5. Set up three local variables called `$verbform`, `$tense_marker` and `$third_sing_suff`, initialise the first two to empty strings and the last one to `'s'`.
6. Based on tests of the different properties stored in `%attributes`, establish the correct forms for the base form of the verb and its potential suffixes, concatenate the verbform, and `return` it.
7. Modify 'test_Verb_obj.pl' appropriately to test the subroutine, each time printing out suitable messages that make it easier to identify what kind of verb form you wanted to produce or which parameter you were changing.

Although this is already a very useful object for generating any regular verb forms, of course it would still be much more useful if we also incorporated a mechanism for handling irregular verbs, which, however, I shall leave to you as a further exercise.

GETTING GRAPHICAL
(SIMPLE USER INTERFACES)

As we have seen repeatedly now, although we can always use <STDIN> and <STDOUT> or create our own filehandles to get input from or write output to, this is not necessarily the most convenient way of interacting with our programs. Especially if you want to process data that is in a special character set, like one of the Unicode formats, it may be difficult or even impossible to use the command line. We may also not necessarily know which action we want to perform on our data next if there is a series of possible options, such as annotating data inside an *annotation editor* and so on. These are all excellent reasons for creating a GUI and thereby presenting the user of the program with an *event-driven* interface. Even though these days there are a number of different *toolkit* modules available for creating GUIs in Perl, the only one we will discuss here is *Perl/Tk*.

12.1 ELEMENTS OF A GUI

The elements that a GUI can be constructed from in Tk are called *widgets* and a Tk-based program generally consists of (at least) one *Main Window* and possibly an additional number of *Toplevel* windows that contain(s) a number of widgets. Another type of container is the *Frame* widget, which allows you to group other widgets together and position them more easily. All widgets are objects that have specific methods and properties associated with them, depending on their function. There are many different types of widgets, ranging from *Labels*, (text) *Entries*, various types of *Buttons* to even fully fledged small *text editors*. We will not have time to discuss all of them, but if you should find yourself creating GUIs frequently and extensively you should probably read *Mastering Perl/Tk* by Steve Lidie and Nancy Walsh. When the Tk module is installed, it also installs with it a widget demo program which you can run by typing widget at the command line. This illustrates most of the different widget types available in the module and also allows you to inspect the sample code for the programs, which you can use for inspiration. Figure 12.1 overleaf only shows a few of the widgets we will be using in our programs:

In Figure 12.1 – which, incidentally, is something we are going to program a little later as a means to test the verbform object we created earlier – you can see a variety of different widgets. The first row of the main window contains a label, an entry widget for providing an infinitive form for a regular verb and a straightforward button to be used to exit the program. The closing function can of course also be achieved through

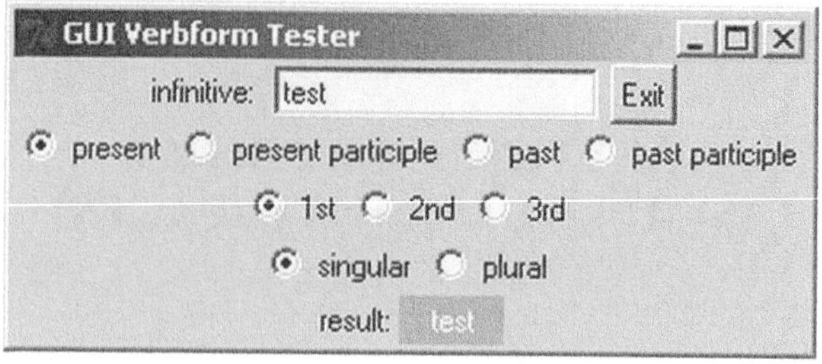

Figure 12.1   The GUI Verbform Tester

the conventional 'x'-button in the main window's *title bar*. The latter, apart from also enabling the user to minimise or maximise the program window, also contains a title string for the program. The next three rows contain a series of *Radiobuttons* that allow the user to set the different properties for the verbform. Note that the options in each row are mutually exclusive, which is exactly the purpose of this type of button. The last row actually contains two labels, the left functioning as a *legend* or explanation for the one on the right, which displays the resulting verbform and is given a different background colour to make it stand out. Now that you have seen an example of a program, let us start discussing the individual steps needed in constructing a GUI in Tk.

12.2 BASIC STEPS IN CREATING TK PROGRAMS

The first thing you need in order to create a Tk-based program is to import the Tk toolkit by adding the use Tk; directive at the top of your program. This will automatically import the most basic widgets, but in some cases you may also have to import some other, more specific, modules. Perl will always warn you, though, if you are trying to use a module that you first need to import. The next step is generally to set up the main window, which can be done in one of two ways, either by explicitly calling the new method of the MainWindow object to create a reference that you store in a scalar variable, usually called $mw, or by calling the tkinit method to assign to the same variable. The two possible alternatives thus look like this:

```
$mw = MainWindow->new();
$mw = tkinit();
```

Of course, you could always include a section containing further module import statements or variable declarations before creating the main window. As a matter of fact, this is probably something that you will definitely end up doing if you want to write applications with more extensive menu systems and other useful features. You can also pass additional arguments to the main window constructor, such as the title that is supposed to appear in the title bar. At creation time, such properties are usually provided in the general key => value style we have previously used for our own argument passing, only that the keys in Tk widgets are normally prefixed by a hyphen, for example -title => 'Test GUI' and so on. Often, these property keys may also have correspondingly named accessor methods that can be used after the object has already been created, such as $mw->title('Another Test GUI');, but this depends on the widget and which properties it exposes in this way.

Next, you add the widgets, or container frames that include the widgets, to your program and position them. Once you have set up the basic layout, you still need to add one more statement to conclude the 'graphics part' of your application. This special statement is simply the command MainLoop;, without which you would not be able to interact with the program because this is what actually makes the Tk window *listen* to *events*, such as mouse clicks, menu selections or user entries, and allows the widgets to react in an appropriate manner. All other interaction with the program is usually conducted through subroutines that you either define in other parts of the program or anonymous ones that you can associate with menu or widget command properties (-command) directly.

[**Exercise 36**] Let us now start designing a simple application step by step, beginning with a bare window as described above:

1. Start by creating a new file called 'first_gui.pl'.
2. Do not forget to add the usual documentation comments at the top, apart from being strict.
3. Import the Tk module.
4. Create the main window using one of the two methods described above.
5. Add the title *First GUI program* to the title bar, either by using the method inside the constructor call or as a separate method invocation on the main window object.
6. Add the event loop.
7. Save and test the program.

The result should look as in Figure 12.2.

Figure 12.2   A bare Tk GUI

12.3 ADDING WIDGETS

To illustrate the basic way of adding to, and displaying other types of widgets in, a main or toplevel window, we will now take a look at how to create one or more buttons inside our main window, which will be its *parent* widget. Let us call the program that allows us to do this 'gui_with_button.pl'. As the button is one of the most basic components in a Tk program, we do not need to specify any additional modules to create one, but simply have to call an appropriate method to create and associate it with its parent. The basic syntax we will use for producing our particular button example is $mw->Button();. [**Exercise 37**] In order to see what happens if we use this syntax, copy the contents of 'first_gui.pl' to 'gui_with_button.pl', adjust the window title appropriately, add the command given above between the statement that creates the main window, but before the MainLoop(); statement, and then run the program to test the result. Now, you may be somewhat surprised to see that – at least apparently – nothing apart from the title has actually changed. This is because, so far, we have only told the Tk module to create the button, but not specified any way to arrange and display it inside the parent window. To achieve the latter, we need to use one of Tk's *geometry management* options that are responsible for controlling Tk layouts. The one we shall exclusively use here is called pack and is simply appended as a method call to whichever widget you want to be positioned and displayed, as in $mw->Button()->pack();. The result of this last statement can be seen in Figure 12.3.

Figure 12.3   A Tk GUI with an unlabelled button

As you can see in Figure 12.3 and of course if you run the modified program your-self, creating and packing the button without any additional options will now display the button centred inside the program window, as well as adjust the GUI window size to the default height of the button. If you click on the button, however, nothing will in fact happen, simply because we have not associated any command with it. Furthermore, we have not even given it a description yet, so nothing appears as the button text either. Let us rectify these things first before we start playing with some alignment options for pack. To make the button really do something and to also display an informative piece of text on it, we will modify the statement that creates and displays it to this: $mw->Button(-text => 'Exit', -command => sub {exit()})->pack();. The -text option will simply associate the button text with it, while the -command option attaches a *callback* or *event handler* with a mouse click on it in form of an *anonymous subroutine*. The anonymous subroutine in our case triggers the exit method of the GUI, which does essentially the same thing as clicking the x in the title bar, that is, to close down the GUI application, although the same effect is in reality produced through different mechanisms. The resulting program should look as in Figure 12.4.

Figure 12.4   A Tk GUI with a labelled button

Modify the program accordingly and then run and test it. Next, let us play around a little with the basic options for pack. These allow us to position (-side, -anchor) the widget, specify whether there should be any additional spacing inside or around it (-ipadx, -ipady; -padx, -pady) or whether it can resize or not (-fill, -expand). Learning how to use these options in more advanced programs will require a fair amount of expertise and probably even more practice, but we will start with some simple options, anyway.

Before we do so, though, let us try to understand the basic idea behind the arrangement scheme. When a widget is added to a parent container, it is first placed within a space referred to as an *allocation rectangle*, due to its rectangular shape. Widgets are added to the container in the order in which they are specified (although it is possible to change this), so each widget is allocated such a rectangular space that it is allowed to occupy. The size of this allocated space depends on which option is chosen for -side in the first instance, because the options left and right will allocate space vertically, while top (the default setting) and bottom will allocate space on the horizontal dimension, respectively. The size of the widget within the allocation space, in the first instance, depends on its physical size, for example, the length of the text on a button or label. This, however, can be changed by using the -fill option, where the possible values are x (horizontal), y (vertical) and both. This option will allow the widget to fill the allocation rectangle in the specified direction, while the -expand option, with its values 0 and 1, will affect the width of the allocation space, allowing it to resize when the user resizes the container widget/window. One further option concerning the placement of widgets is -anchor, which allows you to specify points on the compass, as well as the value center (default).

As all this description is a little abstract, here is a little test program called 'gui_pack_options_tester.pl' that you can use to explore the options and alignment for the sides and test the results.

```
1  use Tk;
2  # create main window
3  my $mw = tkinit(-title => 'GUI Program for Testing
   pack() Options');
4  # define pack options (other than side) for all
   buttons
5  my @opts = qw (-fill y -expand 1);
6  # create the buttons and display them using pack
   with the options array specified above
```

```
7  foreach my $side (qw(top bottom left right)) {
8    # create buttons with alignments as specified in
     the list above
9    $mw->Button(-text => 'Exit '.$side, -command =>
     sub {exit()})
     ->pack(-side => $side,@opts);
10 }
11 MainLoop();
```

You should play around a little with the above program to at least get a rough feeling for how you can manipulate the arrangement and size of widgets. To get an even better impression, try to resize the window in a few directions to observe the effect of the different options you specify. And if you pay close attention to the code, you also ought to be able to see how you can easily 'interpolate' a number of prede-fined options, as well as create a series of similar widgets, efficiently. Now, setting up a few buttons on different sides of a window is still relatively easy, but things can get far more complicated very quickly and that is when we need to start finding other ways of arranging our widgets in order to control their placement. How to do this, as well as getting to know a few more widget types, we will learn now when we start constructing our GUI Verbform Tester.

[Exercise 38] The GUI part of the program – which we will call 'gui_verbform.pl' – consists of a main window that contains five embedded frames that group together the sub-widgets to arrange them in a logical fashion. The first one acts as a toolbar, where we can input an infinitive form as well as exit the program. The second one allows us to select an option for *tense*, the third one for *person*, the fourth one for *number*, and finally one to display the result. In addition to this, we will need to set up an instance of Verb_obj to be used by the program, along with a subroutine that we will call 'show_verbform', which will allow us to retrieve the appropriate arguments to the make_verbform method of the verb object from the user selection in order to update the verbform display on the GUI.

1. Begin by importing the relevant modules.
2. Set up a variable $infinitive and initialise it to test.
3. Create a verb object, initialising the stem to the value of $infinitive.
4. Create another (initially empty) variable called $verbform to hold the final result.
5. Set up suitable default values for *tense*, *person*, and *number*, storing them in cor-respondingly named variables.
6. Create the main window with the title 'GUI Verbform Tester'.
7. Set up an array variable called @side_opts and initialise it to qw (-side left), as most of our widgets will be packed against the left.

Before we can continue writing the rest of the program, though, we first need to discuss a few more widgets, beginning with the Frame. This type of widget allows us to attain the appropriate grouping and packing of the individual rows of buttons inside the main window. A Frame, as it is simply a container for other widgets, is normally invisible, unless you specify some options for it such as -borderwidth or -relief to make it stand out in some way. As frames are generally associated with main windows (or toplevels), the general syntax for creating them is either something like my $toolbar = $mw->Frame; or my $toolbar = $mw ->Frame(...); if you want to specify further options inside the brackets. You may have noticed that my syntax examples here were different from the previous ones, where we simply set up some buttons and associated them with the main window. There, we did not actually create an additional named reference to each Button widget as we did for the Frame this time. The reason for this was that, other than clicking on the buttons to trigger their associated commands, which the main window handles for us, we probably have no further reason to change any of the aspects of these buttons, while we generally still need to have a handle on whatever frames we create in order to be able to associate other widgets with them. Of course, there may also be cases where we may want to change certain features of buttons, for instance if they ought to become disabled once we have clicked on them or for some other possible reason, and then we would probably create an explicit named reference to them, too.

Once we have set up a Frame, we can start associating a number of other widgets to be packed inside it. The additional widgets we shall need for our program – apart from the general type of Button we already know about – are the Label, the Entry and the Radiobutton. In most cases, the Label widget is used as a 'passive' GUI element, simply to provide a legend for the GUI item that appears next to it, as we can see in the two labels 'infinitive:' and 'result:' in the top and bottom rows of our program. We can, however, also use the Label as a means of displaying the result of a computation by linking it to a variable via the -textvariable option. This option takes a reference to a scalar variable as its value, and we will make use of this when we compute any changes to our verbform, as we can simply assign the result of the modification back to the variable $verbform that we already set up above and have any changes automatically reflected in the label next to 'result:' in the bottom row. This Label is also distinguished from the two passive ones through two additional widget attributes, -foreground, which is here set to white, and -background, set to orange, to highlight the result. As the Entry widget, which is a basic text input widget for relatively short text, also has the same -textvariable option, we will simply tie this to $infinitive and can thus get access to the stem.

Radiobuttons are used to specify mutually exclusive options, so they are ideal for our purpose of setting the specific properties of the verbform for *tense, number* or *person*. Each Radiobutton has a label associated with it via the -text option, so we do not need to create extra Label widgets for a series of radiobuttons. All radiobuttons in a series are linked to the same -variable option via a scalar refer- ence, which is similar to the -textvariable option we saw above, but this time the value that will be assigned to that reference when the Radiobutton is clicked comes from the -value option of the button. Armed with this knowledge, we can now continue designing our program.

8. Set up a frame for the toolbar described previously and associate it with `$toolbar`.

9. Add the label 'infinitive: ' for the text entry and pack it using the predefined options array from above.

10. Next, define a variable `$stem_entry` and link the `Entry` widget with it. The options for this should be `-text`, with its value `$infinitive`, and the `-textvariable` linked to a reference to the same variable.

11. Add the exit button with the default alignment options.

12. Pack the toolbar, aligned to the top.

13. Create the three button bar frames for the verbform options, calling them `$frame_` + `tense`, `person` and `number`, respectively.

14. Add the relevant buttons to each frame. To do this in an efficient way, use a similar mechanism to the one I used in lines 7–10 of 'gui_pack_options_tester. pl', providing a list of suitable values to a `foreach` loop. Inside each loop, create the relevant `Radiobuttons`, setting the `-text` and `-value` to the current value inside the loop, and associating the `-variable` option with the appropriate predeclared variable for the particular feature that you want to set with the button. Clicking any one of the buttons should always trigger the same `-command` option, namely, a callback to the `show_verbform` subroutine. To do this, the option needs to be associated with a reference to the subroutine `\&show_verbform`. All buttons should be packed using the default settings.

15. Pack each of the three frames after creating the radiobuttons without providing any particular options to pack.

16. Create a final `Frame`, called `$result_frame`, embed the two remaining labels with any appropriate options and then pack the frame without any specific options. Do not forget to tie the 'active' `Label` to `$verbform`!

17. Before starting the `MainLoop`, add a call to the subroutine to initialise the display.

All that remains to do now is to create the subroutine, which is what we will do next. This should not be particularly difficult in general, but we need to be careful not to forget one particular characteristic of our verb object, which is that we designed it with one special feature, which is that the property values for the participles were abbreviated to `pres. part.` and `past part.`, so that we could be lazy when typing them in on the command line or in our test programs. This, however, would now cause us problems because we set up the GUI in such a way that the value associated with the participle entries corresponds to the full expressions. We also do not use the ordinal (suffix) markers for the object, so those would equally interfere with using the object within the GUI environment. In order to overcome this problem, we need to make sure that, inside the subroutine, we create localised copies of the relevant strings and manipulate them accordingly, so that they can be passed to the object, which will then compute the resulting verbform.

18. Set up the subroutine.

19. Make a localised copy of `$tense`.

20. Check to see whether the localised copy ends in 'participle' and, if so, make sure that any non-abbreviated content is abbreviated properly.

21. Next, make a localised and suitably shortened copy of $person.

22. Use the verb object we created at the beginning of our program to compute a new verbform, based on the values stored in the relevant variables and assign the result back to $verbform.

23. Save and run the program, changing the infinitive a few times and setting the additional properties via the buttons.

The sample program we developed above already demonstrates some of the most important concepts in constructing and creating appropriate layout schemes for GUIs. Apart from this, we have also explored some basic methods of handling user-interaction. However, GUIs in Perl/Tk can be much more powerful and permit the user a much higher degree of interaction, rather than just allowing them to type in simple word stems and click on buttons to see them modified.

12.4 THE GUI CONCORDANCER – AN ADVANCED EXAMPLE

[**Exercise 39**] To illustrate some more advanced interactivity features that will also allow us to save the output of a program, we will now create a more complex program, in fact a re-implementation of our earlier command line-based concordancer as a fully fledged GUI program with a menu bar, an output text widget and enhanced highlighting features for our concordance hits. Starting our description from the top, our concordance program will consist of a Tk Menu, a toolbar that will hold the Entry fields for a search term and the size of the context, and a Text widget that will receive the output. An illustration of the 'final product' is given in Figure 12.5.

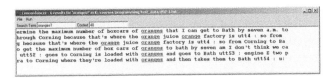

Figure 12.5   The GUI concordancer

The screenshot in Figure 12.5 shows the result of a concordance for the regex search term oranges? in a sample file from the Trains 93 corpus (freely available from <http://www.cs.rochester.edu/research/cisd/resources/trains.html>), with a context of 40 characters on either side of the main hit (displayed in the centre), but where in fact all hits within the context *span* are highlighted in blue and underlined. The latter is a feature of the Text widget, which allows us to *tag* specific ranges of text and apply some predefined formatting to it, which is essentially the same as using *styles* in a word-processor. As you can see, the program's menu bar contains two main menu items, a 'File' and a 'Run' menu. Below the 'File' menu entry (but not visible in the screenshot), there are three further *cascaded* items for 'Load', 'Save Concordance', and 'Exit', which allow us to load a file for concordancing, save the search results displayed in the window, and to close the program. The 'Run' menu item does not contain any sub-menu items, but simply triggers the search. We will begin our discussion of the implementation details by looking at how to construct the Menu.

12.4.1 ADDING A MENU BAR AND THE REMAINING GUI ELEMENTS

The easiest way to set up a menu in Tk is to set up a reference to an anonymous, nested array of menu items that can later be used as the argument to the Menu's −menuitems property. The array that we will use for our concordancer is shown immediately below.

```
1   my $menu_items = [
2       ['Cascade' => '~File', -tearoff => 0,-menuitems
        =>
3           [
4               [Button => '~Load', -command =>
                \&load_file],
5               [Button => '~Save Concordance',
                -command =>
                \&save_concordance],
6               [Button => 'E~xit',-command => sub
                {exit}],
7           ],
8       ],
9       [Button => '~Run', -command =>
            \&do_concordance],
10  ];
```

At the highest level within this array, we either find arrays for simple widget defini-tions (line 9) or Cascade items (line 2) that in turn contain sub-arrays that define arrays of sub-menu items/widgets, which are generally buttons. Inside an item (sub-) array, the first array element specifies the type of widget as a property, while its associ-ated value corresponds to the value that is normally associated with the -text prop-erty, so the widget definition is slightly different from the standard way. As you can see, Cascades also have a -menuitems property whose value is the sub-array of widgets. A menu item at the top level can be triggered via the combination of Alt + a character in the item name that is prefixed by a tilde, as you can see for the '~File' item above. On levels below this, the item can be triggered simply by pressing the character when the Cascade has been opened. This character will also appear underlined. A Cascade can also have a −tearoff property associated with it, which we have here disabled (0) because we do not want the menu item to be undockable.

To use the anonymous array with the menu when we set up the latter (line 1 below), you of course need to have predeclared it. Once the Menu has been created, we call the configure method of the main window, providing the reference to the menu as the value to the −menu property (line 2 below).

```
1   my $menu = $mw->Menu(-menuitems => $menu_items);
2   $mw->configure(-menu => $menu);
```

Please note that the menu does not require packing as this is automatically handled by the program window. The toolbar beneath the menu is set up in exactly the way we discussed in the previous section, so I shall not discuss this further. Just remember to associate the Entry fields with some predeclared variables, ideally called $pattern and $context. However, before we start the MainLoop, we do two more things that require explanation and are first shown below again.

```
1   # set up the text widget for output
2   my $text = $mw->Scrolled('Text',-wrap => 'word',
      -font => '{Courier New} 12 bold',-scrollbars =>
      'osoe')->pack(-side => 'bottom', -anchor => 'w',
      -expand => 1,-fill => 'both');
3   # configure the highlighting for the search term
4   $text->tagConfigure('highlight', -foreground =>
      'blue', -underline => 1);
5   # calculate relative screen height and width for
      sizing the program window
6   my ($width,$height) = (int($mw->screenwidth()*.75),
      int($mw->screenheight()*.50));
7   $mw->geometry($width.'x'.$height.'+10+1');
```

In line 2 above, we set up the Text widget (which previously has to be imported via use Tk::Text;), using the Scrolled method of the main window with some optional (o) horizontal (s) and vertical (e) scrollbars (-scrollbars => 'osoe'). As you can see, we also set the font (-font) and specify that line wrapping should only occur after a word end (-wrap). The Scrolled method can take any widget type that makes sense to scroll as an argument and makes it scrollable, which alleviates us from having to construct the scrollbars manually. To be able to add the highlighting to our search hit in the text window, we use the tagConfigure method of $text to define a tag called 'highlight' in line 4. This tag will later turn the search hits blue and underlined when we insert the concordance lines.

Lines 6 and 7 illustrate how we can specify the position and size of $mw via the geometry method. We first use the screenwidth and screenheight methods of $mw to get the height and width of the output screen and then multiply these by .75 and .5, respectively, to later be able to set the program window to 75 per cent of the screen width and 50 per cent of the screen height. Because the geometry method expects whole numbers as values and the calculations may sometimes return non-integer values, we use the Perl's int function to round them. The '+10+1' in the argument to geometry mean that we want to position the window 10 pixels from the left edge of the screen and 1 pixel from the top, just so that the program is not squashed against the edge of the screen.

12.4.2 PROGRAMMING THE FUNCTIONALITY

Now that we have discussed most of the new elements for the GUI, we only need to create some subroutines that will allow us to interact with the user interface. If you look back at the definition of the menu items above, you will notice that they should be called `load_file`, `do_concordance` and `save_concordance`. Now, since much of the functionality required by these routines is essentially very similar to what we wrote before, I want to leave most of the writing up to you as an exercise, but only explain some of the GUI-specific parts related to file selection, retrieving the contents of $text, error handling and using the highlighting tags in some detail.

Let us start with the file selection mechanism that will be used to retrieve an existing file for concordancing, as well as the almost identical one for specifying a new filename for saving the concordance results. The method for retrieving filenames from the system in Tk is called `getOpenFile`, which opens a file selection dialogue that allows you to navigate through the directories of the operating system to select a file by clicking on it. You will be familiar with this procedure from working with other programs that allow you to open files in this way. The exact look and feel of the dialogue depends on the operating system, so I shall not provide a screenshot here. The method can take a number of different arguments, such as the starting directory (`-initialdir`), a file pattern list (`-filetypes`) in form of an anonymous array (reference) like the one we saw above for the menu items and which allows you to specify pairs of file type names and associated extensions, and the option to define your own title for the dialogue (`-title`). It returns a filename or empty string if the user cancels. Out of these options, we will only use the first one, specifying the current directory as our starting point for the search, thus `my $file = $mw ->getOpenFile(-initialdir => '.');`, but of course you can customise this later.

For the corresponding dialogue for saving the results later, we will use the counterpart to `getOpenFile`, `getSaveFile`. This time, however, we will not actually provide a starting directory, but use the two additional options `-defaultextension`, set to `'txt'`, and `-initialfile`, set to `'concordance.txt'`. The first one will automatically add the extension .txt to the filename if the user does not type it in and the second one will 'suggest' the default output filename 'concordance. txt' to the user, which can of course always be changed.

As far as the error handling in our previous – non-GUI – programs was concerned, we usually either emitted a warning or even closed down the program completely whenever something went wrong because otherwise the program would have possibly hung with an error message. Of course, even in a Tk-based program, programming errors can cause a program to hang, but in order to handle errors, we do not usually want to close the whole program but rather *trap* the error and either do nothing or alert the user, showing a message that something has gone wrong and then simply exit the subroutine that caused the error. There are different types of dialogues available in Perl/Tk for achieving the former, but we will actually use the `messageBox` method for this, whereas the latter can be done by simply using `return` in a *void* context to exit the offending subroutine after the user has confirmed the error, which passes back program control to the `MainLoop`. A screenshot of one of the message boxes for our program is given in the Figure 12.6.

Figure 12.6   A messageBox example

The `messageBox` method has four properties associated with it that can be seen in Figure 12.6, `-title`, `-message`, `-type`, and `-icon`. The first of these allows you to customise the title in the title bar of the message box, the second to specify a more explicit message on the main dialogue body and the third specifies the nature of the dialogue and the buttons that will be displayed on it. This allows the options `'AbortRetryIgnore'`, `'OK'`, `'OKCancel'`, `'RetryCancel'`, `'YesNo'` or `'YesNoCancel'`, which should be relatively self-explanatory. If the user clicks on any of the buttons, the corresponding string value will be returned and you can write program code to react accordingly. In our case, we shall simply use the `'OK'` option to let the user acknowledge the error and then `return` from the subroutine, anyway, so we do not even need to check the return type. Some of the possible values for the `-icon` property are `'error'`, `'info'`, `'question'` and `'warning'`, out of which we shall use the first one. If you want to, you can of course experiment with the other ones to see what they look like. At this point, you should already know enough to be able to create the interface, albeit still with reduced functionality.

1. Create the basic GUI, including the menu bar, the tool bar and the scrolled `Text` widget.
2. Before you try to run the program to test the layout, make sure you at least create the skeletons for the subroutines to avoid any error messages.
3. Implement the error handling along with the `getOpenFile` and `getSave-File` methods for obtaining filenames as discussed above. For the `load_file` routine, it is probably sufficient to simply `return` if the filename is empty, but for `save_concordance` you should definitely alert the user if the filename returned is empty.
4. Now implement the error handling for `do_concordance`. Remember, this needs to verify two things, the presence of a filename and a pattern in the associated `Entry` widget.

5. Finish implementing the load_file routine. This simply involves assigning the contents of $file to $input_file after the error handling stage. As an additional nicety, we can also set the title of the main window to something more informative using the following syntax: $mw->title("Concordancer - ready for $input_file");.

6. Test the implementation up to this point again.

In the next section, we will learn about how to interact with the Text widget, how to write to it, how to style its text, and how to retrieve text from it again.

12.4.3 HANDLING THE TEXT WIDGET

There are essentially three methods for getting text into a Text widget: to type or paste it in yourself; to tie its contents to a filehandle like STDOUT; or to use its insert method. The first should be self-evident and you could test this even now at the current state our application is in. The second is slightly more complex, so we will not discuss it here, but instead concentrate on the third one. Inserting or manipulating text via a subroutine in a GUI application is done by using the insert method with up to three arguments, the index position, a string to insert plus, optionally, a tag name that will determine the formatting of the string. If you do not want to or cannot specify the tag at insertion time, you can always add one later by using the tagAdd method, which takes the name of the tag, a starting index and an end index as arguments. This is in fact the way we shall handle our highlighting later.

Index positions generally consist of strings comprising a line number, followed by a dot and a character position, for instance '1.0' for the beginning of the first line of text. However, index positions do not always need to be expressed in terms of two digits, but can also be provided as named positions or relative to a given index. Examples of named positions would be 'end', which refers to the very last position inside a Text widget, linestart or lineend, which refer to the beginning or end of a given line, respectively, as in '1.linestart', which is equivalent to '1.0' from above. Relative offsets can be specified by providing a base index +/- one of the two options chars or lines. For example, '5.0 - 1 chars' would refer to the last character position at the end of the fourth line or 'end - 2 lines' to the second line prior to the end of the text. To be able to determine the current index position in terms of line and character index, you can use the index method to translate named index positions as in my $index = $text->index('end');, from which you can then extract the sub-parts like this: my ($line_num, $char) = split /\./, $index;. We will need this later to be able to calculate the positions for the highlighting.

Just as we can use index positions to insert text, we can also employ them to retrieve or delete it. Thus, getting the contents of a Text widget is usually achieved like this: my $text_content = $text->get('1.0', 'end');. And if we need to clear the contents of the widget, as we always ought to do before running a new concordance, we can use the same index in conjunction with the delete method, as in $text->delete('1.0', 'end');. Now that we have learnt about all this functionality of the Text widget, we can finally finish writing our concordancer.

1. Start by completing the save_concordance subroutine, based on your knowledge of how to retrieve the contents of the Text widget. Before simply printing
   the contents to a filehandle, though, make sure that you 'highlight' all the matches
   in the output text using the same format we employed before for text output from
   our earlier concordancers.
2. Now, complete the do_concordance routine after the error handling stage.
3. As a first step, clear the contents of $text.
4. Slurp in the file and clean it up as we did before, removing newlines and redundant
   spaces. In addition, also strip out any potential (HTML or XML) markup the file
   may contain. This will also allow us to concordance on web pages.
5. Set up a while loop, like our earlier one, that will allow you to find and store the
   match positions inside the source file and calculate how many hits there were in
   the file.

The next part is nearly identical to the creation of the earlier non-GUI concordance output. This again involves the calculation of the padding, though this time the
value of $context will be based on the value in the corresponding Entry widget
which references $context via its -textvariable property. This way, we can
also adjust the context for our concordance dynamically and rerun the concordance if
the context proves insufficient. Furthermore, once we have extracted the concordance
lines from the file, we cannot simply add the highlighting via a substitution operation.
Instead, we need to calculate the match start and end positions again, only this time
for the extracted result strings, determine the last position inside the Text widget
each time we insert some content, insert the result string, and then apply the highlight tag to the text. And finally, having tagged the output, we also need to add a
newline again. As this part is still fairly complex, I will provide the solution for this
again below.

```
1   for (my $hit = 0;$hit <= $hits-1;$hit++) {
2           my $padding = 0;
3           # extract relevant substring from file
            contents string
4           # starting offset = match position, length
            = length of match + 2 * context
5           # if match position - context is
            negative...
6           my $start = $starts[$hit]-$context;
7           if ($start =~ /^-/x) {
8               $padding = 0-$start;
9               $start = 0;
10          }
11          my $result = substr($file_content,
            $start,$ends[$hit]+ 2 * $context);
12          # determine the position inside the widget
13          my $index = $text->index('end');
```

```perl
14          my ($line_num, $char) = split /\./,
            $index;
15          $line_num--;
16          # determine the match positions again,
            this time inside the result string
17          my (@result_ends,@result_starts) =
            ((),());
18          while ($result =~ /($pattern)/g) {
19                  # save the match because it may be
                    of variable length and we need to
                    know starting point and length to
                    retrieve context
20                  my $match = $1;
21                  # store the length in the end array
22                  push @result_ends, pos ($result);
23                  # store the beginning of the match,
                    so we can compute left context later
24                  push @result_starts, (pos($result)
                    - length($match));
25          }
26          # output the result to the text widget
27          $text->insert('end',$result);
28          # add the highlighting via a tag
29          for (my $i = 0; $i <= $#result_
            starts;$i++) {
30                  my ($start, $end) = ($line_
                    num.'.'.$result_starts[$i],
                    $line_num.'.'.$result_ends[$i]);
31                  $text->tagAdd('highlight',$start,
                    $end);
32          }
33          $text->insert('end', "\n");
34      }
35      # adjust the title again to provide
        information for the search results
36      $mw->title("Concordancer - $hits results for
        '$pattern' in $input_file");
```

Now, copy the above into your program, run and test it with a few different files and words. As you do the copying, try to understand exactly what happens where and also think about whether you could not make the code easier to understand by extracting some parts and storing them in another subroutine instead.

13

CONCLUSION

If you have managed to work all the way through this book (and hopefully also understood everything), then you should by now have reached at least an intermediate stage in programming. You will have learnt how to specify and issue various types of instruction to the computer, control the flow of a program, conduct repetitive operations, store data in and retrieve it from files or various types of data structures (ranging from simple to fairly complex ones), and even construct basic user interfaces.

What I consider far more important, though, is that – with any luck – you will also have gained more than just a basic understanding of what it means to handle linguistic data on the computer. I also hope to have succeeded in conveying to you where the most serious difficulties in such an endeavour lie and that, to be able to produce any analysis routines or programs that are at least half-way accurate and fail-safe, a great deal of effort on the part of the programmer needs to be exerted.

To this end, I have tried to present you with programming exercises from as many different areas of linguistics as possible (at this level) and to discuss all the programming constructs we needed in a linguistics-oriented context to make it easier for you to relate to them, as well as being able to apply them to problems that you as linguists may actually be confronted with in your daily work or studies. Of course, as I have pointed out frequently, most of the programs we ended up creating were either 'toy' programs or at the very least still require a fair degree of improvement or extension to turn them into real linguistic analysis tools, but I suppose one cannot really expect more than this from a course that starts at an absolute beginner's level. However, if I have managed to succeed in accomplishing most of the wishes expressed above, you should now be in a position to plan your own projects independently or extend the ones we worked on, have some idea about how to create the necessary resources (ideally in a modular, easy to reuse fashion), and solve your analysis tasks in a fairly efficient way. If, along the way, you may even have gained some new insights into the nature of linguistic data and have come to appreciate how the computer can help us in arriving at such insights, then all my aims in writing this textbook will have been fulfilled completely.

Appendix A

SAMPLE SOLUTIONS

The sample solutions listed below only comprise those that are not actually presented in full inside the running text. All solutions are headed by the names of the programs they implement, but exclude any author information or creation/modification dates, the shebang line and so forth, in order to save space. The full set of solutions in electronic form can also be downloaded from the accompanying website. Each first solution from a chapter will contain some information indicating the name of the relevant chapter in square brackets.

Exercise 1: swap_gone_wrong.pl [What to Store and How (Basic Data Types)]

```
$A = "you";
$B = "are";
print "before swapping: $A $B\n";
$A = $B;
$B = $A;
print "after swapping: $A $B";
```

Exercise 2: swap_nums.pl

```
$A = 1;
$B = 2;
$temp = "";
print "before swapping: $A $B\n";
$temp = $B;
$B = $A;
$A = $temp;
print "after swapping: $A $B";
```

Exercise 3: swap2.pl

```
@words = ("there","is","a","linguist","here");
print "declarative: $words[0] $words[1] $words[2]
$words[3] $words[4].\n";
print "interrogative: $words[1] $words[0] $words[2]
$words[3] $words[4]?";
```

Exercise 4: print_array.pl

```
@words = ("there", "is", "a" , "linguist", "here");
print "printing the array without interpolation: ",
@words,".\n";
print "printing the interpolated array: @words.\n";
```

Exercise 5: join_array.pl

```
@words = ("there", "is", "a" , "linguist", "here");
$joined = join "\n", @words;
print $joined;
```

Exercise 6: print_hash_test.pl

```
%words = ("word1","there","word2", "is","word3",
"a","word4", "linguist","word5", "here");
print "attempting to print the hash without
interpolation: ", %words,".\n";
print "attempting to print the interpolated hash:
%words.\n";
print "attempting to print the hash using join: ",
join " ",%words;
```

Exercise 7: base_charset_loop [Doing Repetitive Tasks Automatically (Basic *for* Loops)]

```
for ($i = 0;$i < 256;$i++) {
     print $i, " => ", chr($i),"\n";
}
```

Exercise 8: extract_nth_element_concat.pl [Working with Text (Basic String Handling)]

```
$n = shift;
$counter = 0;
$string = 'this is a fairly long test string to test
the hypothesis that every nth letter inside this
string may be an e';
print "test string: ",$string,"\n";
# split the string into its individual characters
@original_array = split //, $string;
@array_wo_spaces = ();
@results = ();
# print for debugging purposes to test whether
splitting was successful
#print join "|", @original_array,"\n";
# remove spaces the inefficient way
foreach $letter (@original_array) {
    if ($letter ne ' ') {
```

```
            push @array_wo_spaces, $letter;
    }
}
# debugging output again
#print join "|", @array_wo_spaces,"\n";
# test loop
$array_len = scalar @array_wo_spaces;
print "here are the results for n = $n:\t";
for ($i=0;$i<$array_len;$i++) {
    if (($i+1)%$n == 0) {
        push @results, $array_wo_spaces[$i];
        if ($array_wo_spaces[$i] eq 'e') {
            $counter++;
        }
    }
}
print join "-", @results;
if ($n == 1) {
    $n = $n."st";
}
elsif ($n == 2) {
    $n = $n."nd";
}
elsif ($n == 3) {
    $n = $n."rd";
}
else {
    $n = $n."th";
}
print "\n$counter 'e's found in every $n position in a
string of length ",scalar @array_wo_spaces;
```

Exercise 9: test_prefixation.pl

```
$prefix = shift;
@bases = @ARGV;
foreach $base (@bases) {
    print $prefix.$base, "\n";
}
```

Exercise 10: test_length.pl

```
($str1,$str2) = (shift,shift);
$final_string = '';
# this way, we can initialise all three variables in
one go
$length1 = $length2 = $final_length = 0;
```

```
$length1 = length $str1;
print "The value of \$str1 is '$str1' and its length
is $length1 characters.\n";
$length2 = length $str2;
print "The value of \$str2 is '$str2' and its length
is $length2 characters.\n";
$final_string = $str1." ".$str2;
$final_length = length $final_string;
print "The length of the final string '$final_string'
is $final_length characters and it is composed of
'$str1' and '$str2'.";
```

Exercise 11: sentence_case.pl

```
@words = ('they','are','linguists');
print "Sentence before subject inversion: "
.ucfirst(join(" ", @words))."."."\n" ;
($words[0], $words[1]) = ($words[1], $words[0]);
print "Sentence after subject inversion: "
.ucfirst(join(" ", @words))."?" ;
```

Exercise 12: file_reading.pl [Working with Stored Data (Basic File Handling)]

```
open $IN, "<:encoding(utf-8)", './first_prog.pl' or
die "unable to open first_prog.pl for reading!\n";
@lines = (<$IN>);
$line_count = 0;
foreach (@lines) {
    $line_count++;
    print $line_count, ":\t",$_;
}
```

Exercise 13: loop_file_reading.pl

```
open $IN, "<:encoding(utf-8)", './first_prog.pl' or
die "unable to open first_prog.pl for reading!\n";
$line_count = 0;
while (<$IN>) {
    $line_count++;
    print $line_count, ":\t",$_;
}
```

Exercise 14: file_copy.pl [Working with Stored Data (Basic File Handling)]

```
($in_file,$out_file) = (shift,shift);
print "opening input file $in_file for reading
...\n";
open $IN, "<:encoding(utf-8)", $in_file or die "unable
to open input file $in_file!\n";
```

```
print "opening output file $out_file for writing
...\n";
open $OUT, ">:encoding(utf-8)", $out_file or die
"unable to open $out_file for writing!";
print "starting copy operation ...\n";
while (<$IN>) {
    print $OUT $_;
}
close $IN;close $OUT;
print "finished copying $in_file to $out_file.";
```

Exercise 15: dir_reading.pl

```
$dir_name = shift;
@files = ();
opendir $DIR, $dir_name or die "unable to open current
directory!\n";
@files = readdir $DIR;
closedir $DIR;
foreach $file (@files) {
    print $file, "\n";
}
```

Exercise 16: make_bk_folder.pl

```
$base_dir = shift;
if (substr($base_dir,-1) ne "/") {
    $base_dir.="/";
}
#print $base_dir;
$backup = $base_dir."backup";
if(mkdir $backup) {
    print "successfully created backup folder\n";
}
else {
    die "unable to create backup folder!";
}
```

Exercise 17: dir_reading_filtered01.pl [Identifying Textual Patterns (Basic and Extended Regular Expressions)]

```
($input_dir,$extension) = (shift,shift);
@files = ();
opendir $DIR, $input_dir or die "unable to open
directory $input_dir!\n";
@files = readdir $DIR;
closedir $DIR;
```

```perl
# iterate over array, filtering out all files with the
given extension and printing them
foreach $file (@files) {
    print $file, "\n" if ($file =~ /\.$extension/);
}
```

Exercise 18: regex_tester.pl

```perl
($string,$pattern) = (shift,shift);
$match = qr /$pattern/;
if ($string =~ /$match/) {
    print "The pattern in >>$match<< matches the
    string >>$string<<.";
}
else {
    print "The pattern in >>$match<< does not match
the string >>$string<<.";
}
```

Exercise 19: syllables.pl

```perl
$word = lc shift;
$v = qr/[aeiou]/;
$c = qr/[bcdfghjklmnpqrstvwxyz]/;
$syll = qr/$c$v$c?/;
#print $syll, "\n";
if($word =~/\b($syll+)\b/) {
    print "The syllable structure fits our language."
}
else {
    print "The syllable structure does not fit our
language."
}
```

Exercise 20: concordance01.pl

```perl
# get arguments off the command line
($pattern, $input_file, $output_file) = @ARGV;
# open input file
open $IN, "<:encoding(utf-8)", $input_file or die
"unable to open $input_file for reading!\n";
# open output file
open $OUT, ">:encoding(utf-8)", $output_file or die
"unable to open $output_file for writing!\n";
# loop over lines
while ($line = <$IN>) {
    # test to see whether the line matches the pattern,
    # also setting up a backreference
```

```perl
    if ($line =~ /($pattern)/x) {
        # write the current line number, the match and
        the line to the output file
        print $OUT $., ", ",$1,": ",$line;
    }
}
# close all filehandles
close $IN; close $OUT;
```

Exercise 21: verbform_tester_re.pl

```perl
$verbform = shift;
$form = "";
$base = "";
if ($verbform =~ /(\w+)s$/) {
    $form = " 3rd person singular";
    $base = $1;
}
elsif($verbform =~ /(\w+)ed$/) {
    $form = " a past participle or past tense form";
    $base = $1;
}
elsif ($verbform =~ /(\w+)ing$/) {
    $form = " an ing form";
    $base = $1;
}
else {
    $form = " an infinitive or non-3rd person singular
form";
    $base = $verbform;
}
print "The verbform is", $form, " and its base is
'".$base."'.";
```

Exercise 22: coherence_exercise.pl [Modifying Textual Patterns (Substitution and Transliteration)]

```perl
$in_file = shift;
$out_file = substr($in_file, 0, -4)."_gap.txt";
open (IN, "<", $in_file) or die "unable to find
$in_file!\n";
open (OUT, ">", $out_file) or die "unable to open
$out_file for writing!";
while ($line = <IN>) {
    $line =~ s/\b[Tt]he\b/ /g;
    $line =~ s/\s+/ /g;
    $line =~ s/^\s*//;
```

```
        print OUT $line, "\n";
}
close IN; close OUT;
```

Exercise 23: concordance02.pl

```
# get arguments off the command line
($pattern, $input_file, $output_file) = @ARGV;
# open input file
open $IN, "<:encoding(utf-8)", $input_file or die
"unable to open $input_file for reading!\n";
# open output file
open $OUT, ">:encoding(utf-8)", $output_file or die
"unable to open $output_file for writing!\n";
# loop over lines
while ($line = <$IN>) {
    # test to see whether the line matches the
pattern,
    # also setting up a backreference
    if ($line =~ /$pattern/x) {
        $line =~ s/($pattern)/>>> $1 <<</gx;
        # write the current line number and the line
        with the match highlighted to the output file
        print $OUT $.,": ",$line;
    }
}
# close all filehandles
close $IN; close $OUT;
```

Exercise 24: concordance03.pl

```
($pattern, $context,$input_file,$output_file) = @ARGV;
(@ends,@starts) = ((),());
open $FILE, "<:encoding(utf-8)", $input_file or die
"unable to open $input_file!\n";
# set input separator to nothing
$/ = undef;
# slurp in file
$file_content = <$FILE>;
close $FILE;

for ($file_content) {
    # remove all newlines and replace them by spaces,
    just in case there are line breaks without spaces
    between words
    s/\n/ /xg;
```

```perl
    # collapse all multiple spaces potentially caused
    by the above into a single one
    s/\p{isSpace}+/ /xg;
}

#print $file_content, "\n";
# iterate over file, finding as many matches as
possible
while ($file_content =~ /($pattern)/gx) {
    # save the match because it may be of variable
    length and we need to know starting point and
    length to retrieve context
    $match = $1;
    # store the length in the end array
    push @ends, length ($match);
    # store the beginning of the match, so we can
    compute left context later
    push @starts, (pos ($file_content)
    - length($match));
}

#open the output file
open $OUT, ">:encoding(utf-8)", $output_file or warn
"unable to open $output_file for writing!\n";
# establish how many elements we have in the array of
hits
$hits = scalar @starts;
# iterate over all hits
for ($hit = 0;$hit <= $hits-1;$hit++) {
    $padding = 0;
    # extract relevant substring from file contents
    string
    # starting offset = match position, length =
    length of match + 2 * context
    # if match position - context is negative...
    $start = $starts[$hit]-$context;
    if ($start =~ /^-/x) {
        $padding = 0-$start;
        $start = 0;
    }
    $result = substr($file_content,$start,$ends[$hit]+
    2 * $context);
    # add 'match highlight'
    $result =~ s/($pattern)/>>> $1 <<</gx;
    print $OUT " " x $padding,$result,"\n\n";
```

```
}
close $OUT;
```

Exercise 25: substitute_html.pl

```
$html_string1 = "This is a <b>test</b> string in html
for <i>testing</i> greediness in substitutions.";
$html_string2 = $html_string1;
print "The original string was:\n\n\t", $html_string1,
"\n\n";
$html_string1 =~ s/<.+>//gx;
$html_string2 =~ s/<.+?>//gx;
print "This is the result of the greedy match
substitution:\n\n\t", $html_string1, "\n\n";
print "This is the result of the non-greedy match
substitution:\n\n\t", $html_string2;
```

Exercise 26: sampa_to_ipa.pl

```
$sampa_string = 'D@lQNbraUn@NgreIlaIn';
$ipa_string = $sampa_string;
$ipa_string =~ tr/IE3@AVQOU:TDSZrN/
\x{026A}\x{025B}\x{025C}\x{0259}\x{0251}\x{028C}\
x{0252}\x{0254}\x{028A}\x{02D0}\x{03B8}\x{00F0}\
x{0283}\x{0292}\x{0279}\x{014B}/;

open $OUT, ">:encoding(utf8)", "./phon_conversion.
txt";
print $OUT "SAMPA string before conversion: ",
$sampa_string,"\n";
print $OUT "IPA string equivalent after conversion: ",
$ipa_string, "\n";
close $OUT;
```

Exercise 27: simple_sort_nums.pl [Getting Things Into the Right Order (Basic Sorting)]

```
@unsorted_words = @ARGV;
@sorted_words = sort {$a <=> $b} @unsorted_words;
foreach $word (@sorted_words) {
    print $word, "\n";
}
```

Exercise 28: simple_vocab.pl

```
@words = ();
@vocab_list = ();
$infile = shift or die "Please provide an input file
name!\n";
```

```
open $IN, "<encoding(utf8)", $infile or die "Unable to
open input file $infile!\n";
while ($line = <$IN>) {
    chomp $line;
    next if($line =~/^\s*$/);
    for ($line) {
        # cater for HTML, XML, etc.
        s/<\/?.+?>/ /g;
        # paired single quotes
        s/\'(.+?)\'/$1/g;
        s/[!.,;:?()"\/]//g;
        s/\s-\s/ /g;
        s/^\s*//;
        s/\s+$//;
    }
    @elements = split /\s+/, $line;
    push @words, @elements;
}
close $IN;
@words = sort @words;
foreach $word (@words) {
    print $word, "\n";
}
$array_length = scalar @words;
for ($i = 0; $i < $array_length; $i++) {
    ($a, $b) = ($words[$i], $words[$i+1]);
    if($a ne $b) {
        push @vocab_list, $a;
    }
}

print "\n\nvocab:\n\n";
foreach $word (@vocab_list) {
    print $word, "\n";
}
```

Exercise 29: freq_list.pl

```
%words = ();
# get the flag
$flag = shift;
# test to see whether the first argument was a correct
flag, else print usage
die "Flag required for output file type: -l for
'vocabulary' list, -f for frequency list\n." if ($flag
!~/^-[fl]$/);
```

```perl
$in_file = shift or die "Please provide an input file
name!\n";
# generate the output filename, based on the flag
$out_file ='';
# the following assumes that there is only a single,
three-character extension
if ($flag eq '-l') {
    $out_file = substr($in_file, 0, -3)."lst";
}
else {
    $out_file = substr($in_file, 0, -3)."frq";
}
# process the file
open $IN, "<:encoding(utf8)", $in_file or die "Unable
to open input file $in_file for reading!\n";
while ($line = <$IN>) {
    chomp $line;
    next if($line =~/^\s*$/);
    # clean the line
    for ($line) {
        # cater for HTML, XML, etc.
        s/<\/?.+?>/ /g;
        # paired single quotes
        s/\'(.+?)\'/$1/g;
        s/[!.,;:?()"\/]//g;
        s/\s-\s/ /g;
        s/^\s*//;
        s/\s+$//;
    }
    # get the words
    @elements = split /\s+/, $line;
    foreach $word (@elements) {
        $words{$word}++;
    }
}
close $IN;
# now create the output
open $OUT, ">:encoding(utf8)", $out_file or die
"Unable to open output file $out_file for writing!\n";
if ($flag eq '-l') {
    # alphabetically sorted
    foreach $word (sort keys %words) {
        print $OUT $word,"\n";
    }
}
```

```
else {
    # sorting first in descending frequency order and
    then alphabetically
    foreach $word (sort {$words{$b} <=> $words{$a} ||
    $a cmp $b} keys %words) {
        print $OUT $word, "\t", $words{$word},"\n";
    }
}
close $OUT;
```

Exercise 30: simple_translator_buggy.pl [More Repetitiveness or How to Tie Things Together (Introducing Modularity)]

```
%dict = (
    there => 'dort',
    is => 'ist',
    a => 'ein',
    linguist => 'Sprachwissenschaftler',
    );
$sentence = 'there is a linguist';
foreach $word (split / /, $sentence) {
    $translation .= &dictionary_lookup($word)." ";
    $original .= $word." ";
}
$translation = substr $translation, 0, -1;
$original = substr $original, 0, -1;
print "English: $sentence => German: $translation
\noriginal: $original ???";
sub dictionary_lookup {
    $word = shift;
    $equivalent = $dict{$word};
    $word = $equivalent;
    return $equivalent
}
```

Exercise 31: simple_translator.pl (corrected version using localised variables)

```
use strict;
my $original = "";
my $translation = "";
my %dict = (
    there => 'dort',
    is => 'ist',
    a => 'ein',
    linguist => 'Sprachwissenschaftler',
    );
my $sentence = 'there is a linguist';
```

```perl
foreach my $word (split / /, $sentence) {
    $translation .= &dictionary_lookup($word)." ";
    $original .= $word." ";
}
$translation = substr $translation, 0, -1;
$original = substr $original, 0, -1;
print "English: $sentence => German: $translation
\noriginal: $original";
sub dictionary_lookup {
    my $word = shift;
    $equivalent = $dict{$word};
    $word = $equivalent;
    return $equivalent
}
```

Exercise 32: sample_dict.pl

```perl
use strict;
use utf8;

die "Please input a headword and a property (separated
by a space) to retrieve!\n" if (scalar @ARGV < 2);
my ($word,$property) = @ARGV;

my %dict = (
    house => {
        pos => [qw (NN V)],
        pron => [qw (haʊs haʊz)],
        def => ['A type of building that people live
in.','The act of accommodating s.o. inside a house.'],
        ex => ['My friends recently bought a very nice
house in the countryside.','The refugee camp houses
people from many different countries around the
world.'],
    },
    castle => {
        pos => 'N',
        pron => 'kɑːsɫ',
        def => 'A fortified building where kings,
noble or rich people live.',
        ex => 'My home is my castle.',
    },
);

die "Word >>>$word<<< doesn't exist in dictionary!\n"
if (!exists $dict{$word});
```

```perl
die "Property >>>$property<<< not defined for
>>>$word<<<!\n" if (!exists $dict{$word}{$property});

open my $OUT, ">:encoding(utf8)", './dict_test.txt' or
die "unable to open output file for writing!\n";
print $OUT &get_property($word,$property);
close $OUT;

sub get_property {
    my ($word, $property) = @_;
    my $ref_type = ref $dict{$word}{$property};
    if ($ref_type eq 'ARRAY') {
        my $num = 0;
        my $property_string = '';
        foreach my $prop_element (@{$dict{$word}
{$property}}) {
            $num++;
            $property_string .= $num."\t".
$prop_element."\n";
        }
        chomp $property_string;
        return $property_string;
    }
else {
        return $dict{$word}{$property};
    }
}
```

Exercise 33: Html_handler.pm

```perl
package Html_handler;

use strict;
use LWP::Simple;
use Exporter;

our @ISA = qw (Exporter);
our @EXPORT = qw (&fetch_page &extract_headings
&extract_paragraphs &read_page &return_elements);

my %page_elements = (
   headings => [],
   paragraphs => [],
   );

my $file_content = '';
```

```perl
sub fetch_page {
    my $url = shift;
    my $local_file = $url;
    for ($local_file) {
        s|^\w+?:/+||x;
        # remove any trailing slashes
        s|/$||;
        s|/|__|g;
    }
    # add html if no extension present
    if ($local_file !~ /html?$/) {
        $local_file = $local_file.'.html';
    }
    # create directory for downloads or abort
    if (!-e './downloads') {
        mkdir './downloads' or die "unable to create
downloads directory!";
    }
    $local_file = './downloads/'.$local_file;
    # attempt to get the page
    my $status = getstore($url, $local_file);
    # inform us as to whether the download was
    possible...
    if (is_success($status)) {
        print "OK";
    }
    # ... or not
    else {
        warn "Download for $url failed. Error number:
        ", $status,"\n";
    }
}


sub read_page {
    my $page = shift || './downloads/test__test.html';
    (my $file_name = $page) =~ s/html*$/txt/;
    #print $file_name, "\n";
    # set slurp mode
    $/ = undef;
    open my $IN, "<:encoding(utf-8)", $page or warn
    "unable to open $page for reading!\n";
    $file_content = <$IN>;
    close $IN;
    # check for charset definition
```

```
    $file_content =~ /charset=(.+?)["']/x;
    my $charset = lc $1;
    #print $charset,"\n";
    # re_read if the character set was not UTF-8
    if ($charset ne 'utf-8') {
        open my $IN, "<:encoding($charset)", $page or
        warn "$charset not supported!\n";
        $file_content = <$IN>;
        close $IN;
    }
    # reset input record separator
    $/ = "\n";
}

sub extract_headings {
    while ($file_content =~ m|< (h\d) (?:[^>]+?)?>
    (.+?) <\/ \1 >|xgs) {
        push @{$page_elements{headings}},
        &clean_element_contents($2);
    }
}

sub extract_paragraphs {
    while ($file_content =~ m|< (p) (?:[^>]+?)?> (.+?)
    <\/ \1 >|xgs) {
        push @{$page_elements{paragraphs}},
        &clean_element_contents($2);
    }
}

sub clean_element_contents {
    my $text = shift;
    $text =~ s|</?.+?>||sg;
    return $text;
}

sub return_elements {
    my $element_type = shift;
    return @{$page_elements{$element_type}};
}

1;
```

Exercise 34: Verb_obj.pm [Objects]

```
    package Verb_obj;
```

```perl
use strict;

# constructor
sub new {
    my $class = shift;
    my %args = @_;
    my $self = {
        stem => $args{'stem'},
        person => $args{'person'} || "1",
        tense => $args{'tense'} || 'present',
        number => $args{'number'} || 'singular',
    };
    die "usage: stem => <stem> [person => <1|2|3>
    number => <singular|plural> tense =>
    <present|past|past part.|pres. part.>]!\n"
    if (!defined $self->{'stem'});
    bless $self, $class;
    return $self;
}

# acessor methods
sub get_prop {
    my ($self,$prop) = @_;
    return $self->{$prop};
}

sub set_prop {
    my ($self,$prop,$value) = @_;
    $self->{$prop} = $value;
}

sub make_verbform {
    my $self = shift;
    # interpolate remaining arguments into hash for
    easier access
    my %attributes = ( @_ );
    # build up verbform
    # if no parameters exist, assume that we need to
    get them from the object
    foreach my $key (qw (stem person tense number)) {
        if (!exists $attributes{$key}) {
                $attributes{$key} = $self->{$key};
        }
    }
    my $verbform = '';
```

```perl
    my $tense_marker = '';
    my $third_sing_suff = 's';
    # handle simple cases, final <e> stem, and final
    <sh|ch> separately
    # if we have any past form, including the
    participle, set the tense marker to 'ed'
    if($attributes{'tense'} =~ /past/) {
        if($attributes{'stem'} =~ /e$/x) {
                $tense_marker = 'd';
        }
        else {
                $tense_marker = "ed";
        }
    }
    # if we have a pres. part. instead, set the tense
    marker to 'ing'
    elsif($attributes{'tense'} eq "pres. part.") {
        if($attributes{'stem'} =~ /e$/x) {
                $attributes{'stem'} = substr
                $attributes{'stem'}, 0,-1;
        }
        $tense_marker = "ing";
    }
    # 'add' everything together
    # handle third person singular
    if ($attributes{'tense'} eq 'present' and
    $attributes{'person'} eq '3' and
    $attributes{'number'} eq 'singular') {
        if($attributes{'stem'} =~ /[cs]h$/x) {
                $third_sing_suff = 'es';
        }
        $verbform =
$attributes{'stem'}.$tense_marker.$third_sing_suff;
    }
    else {
        $verbform = $attributes{'stem'}.$tense_marker;
    }
    return $verbform;
}


1;
```

Exercise 35: test_Verb_obj.pl

```perl
  use strict;
```

```perl
use Verb_obj;

my $stem = shift;

my $verb1 = Verb_obj->new('stem' => $stem);
#print $verb1->{'stem'}, "\n";
print "testing setting of default 'person' for
\$verb1: ", $verb1->{'person'}, "\n";
print "testing generation of different (non-object)
verbforms:\n";
print "\t->",$verb1->make_verbform('stem' => 'fear',
'person' => '2'), "\n";
print "\t->",$verb1->make_verbform('stem' => 'bore',
'person' => '3', 'tense' => 'past'), "\n";
print "\t->",$verb1->make_verbform('stem' => 'bore',
'person' => '3', 'tense' => 'present'), "\n";
print "\t->",$verb1->make_verbform('stem' => 'bore',
'person' => '3', 'tense' => 'pres. part.'), "\n";
print "\t->",$verb1->make_verbform('stem' => 'bore',
'person' => '3', 'number' => 'plural', 'tense' =>
'present'), "\n";
print "testing changing object property:\n";
print "setting 'person' to '3(rd)':\n";
$verb1->set_prop('person' => '3');
print "\t->",$verb1->make_verbform(), "\n";
print "setting 'tense' to 'pres. part.':\n";
$verb1->set_prop('tense' => 'pres. part.');
print "\t->",$verb1->make_verbform();
```

Exercise 36: first_gui.pl

```perl
use strict;
use Tk;
my $mw = tkinit(-title => 'First GUI Program');
MainLoop();
```

Exercise 37: gui_with_button.pl

```perl
use strict;
use Tk;

# create main window
my $mw = tkinit(-title => 'GUI Program for Testing
pack() Options');
# define pack options (other than side) for all
buttons
my @opts = qw (-fill y -expand 1);
```

```
# create the buttons and display them using pack with
the options array specified above
foreach my $side (qw(top bottom left right)) {
    # create buttons with alignments as specified in
    the list above
    $mw->Button(-text => 'Exit '.$side, -command =>
    sub {exit()})->pack(-side => $side,@opts);
}
MainLoop();
```

Exercise 38: gui_verbform.pl

```
use strict;
use Tk;
use Verb_obj;

# set up 'dummy' verb object
my $infinitive = 'test';
my $verb = Verb_obj->new('stem' => $infinitive);
# final result is saved in here and linked via
reference to the label to display it
my $verbform = '';
# these will automatically set the defaults for the
radiobuttons
my ($tense, $person, $number) = ('present',
'1st','singular');
# main GUI window
my $mw = MainWindow->new(-title => 'GUI Verbform
Tester');
my @side_opts = qw (-side left);
# 'toolbar'
my $toolbar = $mw->Frame;
$toolbar->Label(-text => 'infinitive:')->pack(
@side_opts);
my $stem_entry = $toolbar->Entry(-text => $infinitive,
-textvariable => \$infinitive)->pack(@side_opts,
qw / -padx 5/);
$toolbar->Button(-text => 'Exit', -command => sub
{exit(0);})->pack(@side_opts);
$toolbar->pack(qw /-side top/);
# tense options, mutually exclusive
my $frame_tense = $mw->Frame;
foreach ('present', 'present participle', 'past',
'past participle') {
  $frame_tense->Radiobutton(-text => $_, -value => $_,
```

```
    -variable => \$tense, -command => \&show_verbform)
  ->pack(@side_opts);
  }

$frame_tense->pack;
# person options, mutually exclusive
my $frame_person = $mw->Frame;
foreach (qw /1st 2nd 3rd/) {
  $frame_person->Radiobutton(-text => $_, -value =>
  $_, -variable => \$person, -command => \&show_
  verbform)->pack(@side_opts);
}
$frame_person->pack();
# number options, mutually exclusive
my $frame_number = $mw->Frame;
foreach (qw /singular plural/) {
  $frame_number->Radiobutton(-text => $_, -value =>
  $_, -variable => \$number, -command => \&show_
  verbform)->pack(@side_opts);
}
$frame_number->pack();
# result display
my $result_frame = $mw->Frame();
$result_frame->Label(-text => 'result:')->pack(
@side_opts);
$result_frame->Label(-textvariable => \$verbform,
-padx => 10, -foreground => 'white', -background =>
'orange')->pack;
$result_frame->pack;
# initialise result display
&show_verbform;
# start event loop
MainLoop();

sub show_verbform {
  # we need to create local copies of all parameters
  to modify because otherwise the radiobuttons do not
  display properly
  my $tense = $tense;
  if($tense =~ /participle$/) {
    $tense =~ s/participle/part./x;
    $tense =~ s/^present/pres./x;
  }
  my $person = substr $person,0,-2;
  $verbform = $verb->make_verbform(stem =>
```

```perl
$infinitive,tense => $tense,number => $number,person
=> $person);
}
```

Exercise 39: gui_concordancer.pl

```perl
use strict;
use Tk;
use Tk::Text;

# concordance parameters
my $context = 40;
my $input_file = '';
my $pattern;
# default packing options
my @pack_opts = qw (-side left);
# anon. array of menu items
my $menu_items = [
    ['Cascade' => '~File', -tearoff => 0,-menuitems =>
        [
            [Button => '~Load', -command =>
            \&load_file],
            [Button => '~Save Concordance', -command
            => \&save_concordance],
            [Button => 'E~xit',-command => sub
            {exit}],
        ],
    ],
    [Button => '~Run', -command => \&do_concordance],
];
# create main window
my $mw = tkinit(-title => 'Concordancer');
# add the menu and configure it to use the menuitems
array from above
my $menu = $mw->Menu(-menuitems => $menu_items);
$mw->configure(-menu => $menu);
# add the toolbar with two entry boxes and associated
labels
my $toolbar = $mw->Frame();
$toolbar->Label(-text => 'Search Term')->pack(
@pack_opts);
$toolbar->Entry(-textvariable => \$pattern)->pack(
@pack_opts);
$toolbar->Label(-text => 'Context')->pack(@pack_opts);
$toolbar->Entry(-textvariable => \$context)->pack(
@pack_opts);
```

```perl
$toolbar->pack(-anchor => 'nw');
# set up the text widget for output
my $text = $mw->Scrolled('Text',wrap => 'word',-font
=> '{Courier New} 12 bold',-scrollbars => 'osoe')
->pack(-side => 'bottom', -anchor => 'w',-expand =>
1,-fill => 'both');
# configure the highlighting for the search term
$text->tagConfigure('highlight', -foreground =>
'blue', -underline => 1);
# calculate relative screen height and width for
sizing the program window
my ($width,$height) = (int($mw->screenwidth()*.75),int
($mw->screenheight()*.50));
$mw->geometry($width.'x'.$height.'+10+1');
# run it
MainLoop();
# subroutines from here...
sub load_file {
   # use the getOpenFile dialogue to ask for an input
filename; starting point is the current directory
   my $file = $mw->getOpenFile(-initialdir => '.');
   # if the user has cancelled the dialogue...
   if ($file eq '') {
       # simply return to the main program
       return;
   }
   # if we have a valid filename...
   # set the input file
   $input_file = $file;
   # adjust the title bar to be a little more
informative
   $mw->title("Concordancer - ready for $input_file");
}

sub do_concordance {
   # error handling for non-existent filenames or
patterns
   if ($input_file eq '') {
       # error message via messageBox
       $mw->messageBox(-title => 'File Name Error',
           -message => 'Please specify an input file
           name!',
           -type => 'OK',
           -icon => 'error'
           );
```

```
    # return to main program
    return;
}
if ($pattern eq '') {
    $mw->messageBox(-title => 'Pattern Error',
        -message => 'Please specify a regular
        expression pattern!',
        -type => 'OK',
        -icon => 'error'
        );
    return;
}
# clear the contents of the text widget
$text->delete('1.0','end');
# get the file contents
open my $FILE, "<:encoding(utf-8)", $input_file or
die "unable to open $input_file!\n";
# set input separator to nothing
$/ = undef;
# slurp in file
my $file_content = <$FILE>;
close $FILE;
# clean the file contents
for ($file_content) {
# remove all newlines and replace them by spaces,
just in case there are line breaks without spaces
between words
s/\n/ /g;
# strip out any markup
s/<.+?>//g;
# collapse all multiple spaces potentially caused
by the above into a single one
s/\s+/ /g;
}
#start the search procedure
my (@ends,@starts) = ((),());
# iterate over file, finding as many matches as
possible
while ($file_content =~ /($pattern)/g) {
# save the match because it may be of variable
length and we need to know starting point and
length to retrieve context
my $match = $1;
# store the length in the end array
push @ends, length ($match);
```

```perl
# store the beginning of the match, so we can
compute left context later
push @starts, (pos($file_content) - length($match));
}
# establish how many elements we have in the array
of hits
my $hits = scalar @starts;
# iterate over all hits
for (my $hit = 0;$hit <= $hits-1;$hit++) {
my $padding = 0;
# extract relevant substring from file contents
string
# starting offset = match position, length = length
of match + 2 * context
# if match position - context is negative...
my $start = $starts[$hit]-$context;
if ($start =~ /^-/x) {
    $padding = 0-$start;
    $start = 0;
}
my $result = substr($file_
content,$start,$ends[$hit]+ 2 * $context);
# determine the position inside the widget
my $index = $text->index('end');
my ($line_num, $char) = split /\./, $index;
$line_num--;
# determine the match positions again, this time
inside the result string
my (@result_ends,@result_starts) = ((),());
while ($result =~ /($pattern)/g) {
    # save the match because it may be of variable
    length and we need to know starting point and
    length to retrieve context
    my $match = $1;
    # store the length in the end array
    push @result_ends, pos ($result);
    # store the beginning of the match, so we can
    compute left context later
    push @result_starts, (pos($result) - length
    ($match));
}
# output the result to the text widget
$text->insert('end',$result);
# add the highlighting via a tag
```

```perl
    for (my $i = 0; $i <= $#result_starts;$i++) {
        my ($start, $end) =
        ($line_num.'.'.$result_starts[$i],$line_
        num.'.'.$result_ends[$i]);
        $text->tagAdd('highlight',$start, $end);
    }
    $text->insert('end', "\n");
    }
    # adjust the title again to provide information for
    the search results
    $mw->title("Concordancer - $hits results for
    '$pattern' in $input_file");
}
sub save_concordance {
    # use the getSaveFile dialogue to get an output
    filename; initial filename is suggested
    my $output_file = $mw->getSaveFile(-
    defaultextension => 'txt', -initialfile =>
    'concordance.txt');
    # error handling on cancel...
    if ($output_file eq '') {
    $mw->messageBox(-title => 'File Name Error',
        -message => 'Please specify a file name for
        output!',
        -type => 'OK',
        -icon => 'error'
        );
    return;
    }
    # open the output file
    open my $OUT, ">:encoding(utf8)", $output_file or
    warn "unable to open output file for writing!\n";
    # retrieve the content from the text widget
    my $text_content = $text->get('1.0','end');
    # add the highlighting
    $text_content =~ s/($pattern)/>>> $1 <<</g;
    # print it out
    print $OUT $text_content;
    # close the handle again
    close $OUT;
}
```

HOW TO GET FURTHER HELP ON PERL

As Perl is a highly popular programming language, there are many resources available, both in form of introductory or advanced-level books, as well as on the internet. The only disadvantage for beginners in our profession is that they are usually not very 'linguistics-oriented'.

As far as standard reference books on Perl are concerned, I would always recommend the ones published by O'Reilly, some of which you can also find in the references section. These are generally written by Perl experts who have also been actively involved in developing Perl, including Larry Wall, the inventor of Perl himself. Explicitly language or linguistics-oriented are Hammond (2003) and Nugues (2006). However, the first – to my mind – has the drawback that not all the examples are linguistically interesting, there seems to be a certain emphasis on designing small experiments, and the syntax is often somewhat quirky. The second one, in contrast, is perhaps aimed more at people who work in natural language processing and therefore tend to have more programming experience. And, while it certainly deals with fairly challenging topics, it also tends to favour Prolog over Perl implementations for the more interesting tasks.

As a quick reference mechanism while you are writing your programs, you can exploit Perl's built-in documentation, which can always be accessed via the perldoc command on the command line if Perl has been installed properly. For a general overview of the individual information 'packages', you can simply say perldoc perl. Once you have identified a particular topic of interest, you can call perldoc again with the name of this special topic, for instance perldoc perlrequick for accessing the quick start reference on regular expressions. If you need information on a specific function or module, you can type perldoc -f *function name* or perldoc *module name*, respectively. And if you want to search for a particular topic in the built-in FAQ, type perldoc -q + a suitable regex. As already pointed out in section 1.5.2., ActivePerl has an additional, highly useful feature, namely that it provides the Perl documentation in HTML format, which is much nicer to read than the command line output, apart from allowing you to check quickly whether a particular module is installed on your computer.

There is also a wealth of Perl resources on the internet and any sensibly phrased internet search on a particular problem you encounter will most probably help you find an adequate solution or at least one that you can use as a starting point for your own endeavours. Failing this, you can always try getting information through the relevant newsgroups for Perl (<comp.lang.perl>) or Perl/Tk (<comp.lang.perl. tk>). You can either just subscribe to them to read about solutions that other people enquire about, or even post your own queries, which will usually be answered by a benevolent 'guru', provided that you have looked at the relevant FAQs first.

REFERENCES

Baker P., A. Hardie and T. McEnery (2006), *A Glossary of Corpus Linguistics,* Edinburgh: Edinburgh University Press.

Biber, D. (1988), *Variation across Speech and Writing,* Cambridge: Cambridge University Press.

Bradley, N. (1998), *The XML Companion,* Harlow: Addison-Wesley.

Burke, S. (2002), *Perl & LWP,* Sebastopol, CA: O'Reilly.

Conway, D. (2005), *Perl Best Practices,* Cambridge: O'Reilly.

Friedl, J. (2006), *Mastering Regular Expressions,* 3rd edn, Cambridge: O'Reilly.

Hammond, Michael (2003), *Programming for Linguists: Perl for Language Researchers,* Oxford: Blackwell.

Kennedy, G. (1998), *An Introduction to Corpus Linguistics,* London: Longman.

Lidie, S., and N. Walsh (2002), *Mastering Perl/Tk,* Sebastopol, CA: O'Reilly.

Nugues, P. (2006), *An Introduction to Language Processing with Perl and Prolog,* Berlin: Springer.

Orwant, J., J. Hietaniemi and J. Macdonald (1999), *Mastering Algorithms with Perl,* Sebastopol, CA: O'Reilly.

Ray, E., and J. McIntosh (2002), *Perl & XML,* Sebastopol, CA: O'Reilly.

Stubblebine, T. (2007), *Regular Expression Pocket Reference,* 2nd edn, Sebastopol, CA: O'Reilly.

Wall, L. (2007), 'Natural Language Principles in Perl', <http://www.wall.org/~larry/natural.html>, last accessed: 26 February 2009, 14:30.

Wall, L., T. Christiansen and J. Orwant (2000), *Programming Perl,* 3rd edn, Sebastopol, CA: O'Reilly.

INDEX

171